Basic Listening for the Classroom

Before HearSay

David Hough

Before Hearsay

Editorial director: Joanne Dresner
Executive editor: Elinor Chamas
Development editor: Claire V. Smith
Assistant editor: Jessica Miller
Test design adaptation: Beckwith-Clark, Inc.
Cover design: Marshall Henrichs
Text art: Dave Sullivan
Production: James Gibbons

ISBN 0-201-60761-1

1 2 3 4 5 6 7 8 9 10-CRS-9998979695

Before HearSay is dedicated to the loving memory of Gary Wood, a caring TESOL professional and close personal friend.

Contents

Preface

Shortly after writing **HearSay**, I attended a language teaching conference in Singapore, the theme of which was classroom discourse. I was very interested in finding ways in which text-book writers could help students to maximize real communication time in the classroom. On my way back to Japan, I visited a very small Iban village in Sarawak on the island of Borneo. There, in a tiny four-room primary school, I found the walls literally covered with student-centered classroom language. Enough, in fact, to enable the students to arrange desks, chairs, books, writing materials, and themselves for a variety of student-centered learning activities, to give directions, ask and answer questions, and manage most classroom interactions.

It was this observation that, upon my return to Japan, inspired me to begin incorporating classroom language into my core teaching materials. Over the next five years, I developed and classroom-tested the language that appears in this text.

Before HearSay attempts to teach these skills in a listening comprehension mode. As such it is both a practical first-encounter classroom skills and pre-survival-level listening compre-hension text which assumes only the most rudimentary knowledge of the English alphabet. Designed for young adult and adult entry-level and false beginner learners of English, it begins by using visual, orthographic, and sound correspondences to impart meaning. Vocabulary is con-textualized in easy-to-understand units with immediate practical application. Sound changes at the word and phrase level are systematically introduced from the first unit. These natural speech patterns are also used to help facilitate the acquisition of key grammatical forms without refer-ence to structure rules.

It is the hope of the author that both students and teachers will find **Before Hearsay** an en-joyable and useful classroom tool.

Acknowledgements: The author would like to thank Jonathan Carpenter, Claire V. Smith, and Ellie Chamas for their valuable advice and assistance, and the teachers in the Iban village of Lundu Sungeu Kayan in Sarawak, East Malaysia for their inspiration.

Guide for teachers

Getting Ready

Each unit begins on a right-hand page with a situational/contextualized unit title, followed by a thematic picture and an introductory exercise. The exercise is intended to give visual and orthographic as well as phonological access to the key vocabulary and structures in the unit. Students are required to listen and point/repeat and not to write.

Listening tasks

Play the tape for each of these tasks. They build on communicative classroom language that has been introduced either in the unit or in previous units. All tasks combine listening with active reinforcement activities such as pointing, repeating, circling, checking, underlining, matching, writing, drawing, and following directions. Please note that in each unit only the "Getting Ready" exercise is recorded twice on the cassette. Where students are called upon to listen two or three times, it is necessary to rewind the cassette to the beginning of the exercise.

Slow and fast speech

The material being taught in the unit is presented here in a phonological breakdown of the key reductions and assimilations that appear in the Tasks which have already been done in the unit. It helps students internalize the sound pattern of English for listening comprehension purposes, and for optional production. In this section the tape can be played as many times as necessary.

Pair work

This is generally a four-part activity. In part one, student A dictates to student B and then checks the dictation. In part two, student A asks student B questions; student B then answers. In some cases, this is an information gap exercise. During these first two parts, student B either has the book closed or is working on the last page of the unit. In parts three and four, the roles are reversed, and student B dictates, checks the dictation, and asks student A questions.

1

Listen and write.

Getting Ready

Listen and point.

Listen		Point	
Repeat		Circle	
Ask		Answer	
Write	ABC	Don't Write	
Read	- - - - -ABC	Match	A d B a C f

Listen and repeat.

TASK 1

Listen and repeat.

1. Point
2. Listen
3. Circle
4. Write
5. Read

6. Match
7. Don't write
8. Ask
9. Repeat
10. Answer

TASK 2

Listen and circle.

	A	B	C
1.	Listen	Repeat	Circle
2.	Answer	Point	Match
3.	Listen	Don't write	Repeat
4.	Write	Don't write	Read
5.	Match	Answer	Read
6.	Ask	Answer	Match
7.	Match	Ask	Write
8.	Ask	Answer	Circle
9.	Circle	Read	Write
10.	Read	Write	Don't write

TASK 3

Listen and circle.

	A	B	C
1.	Listen and point.	Listen and circle.	Listen and repeat.
2.	Read and ask.	Read and write.	Read and answer.
3.	Point and ask.	Point and repeat.	Point and read.
4.	Ask and answer.	Ask and write.	Ask and circle.
5.	Listen and circle.	Listen and write.	Listen and match.
6.	Listen and repeat.	Listen and circle.	Listen and point.

TASK 4

Listen and circle.

	A	B	C
1.	(write)	don't write	repeat
2.	circle	write	don't write
3.	write	read	repeat
4.	match	ask	answer
5.	answer	ask	repeat
6.	listen	read	answer

TASK 5

Slow and fast speech. Listen and repeat.

		Slow	*Fast*
1.	and	[ɛnd]	[n]
		and	'n
		Listen and point.	Lis'n 'n point.
		Listen and repeat.	Lis'n 'n repeat.
		Listen and circle.	Lis'n 'n circle.
		Listen and match.	Lis'n 'n match.
		Listen and write.	Lis'n 'n write.
2.	don't	[dont]	[don]
		don't	don'
		Don't write.	Don' write.

TASK 6

Listen and point.

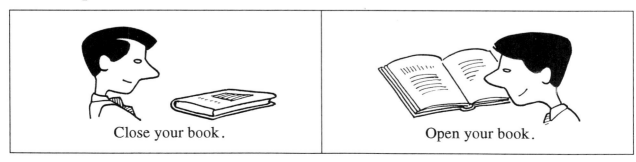

| Close your book. | Open your book. |

Listen and circle.

	A	B
1.	(Close your book.)	Open your book.
2.	Close your book.	Open your book.
3.	Close your book.	Open your book.
4.	Close your book.	Open your book.
5.	Close your book.	Open your book.
6.	Close your book.	Open your book.

TASK 7

Listen and circle.

	A	B
1.	(Close your book.)	Open your book.
2.	Close your book and write.	Close your book and repeat.
3.	Open your book and read.	Open your book and repeat.
4.	Close your book and repeat.	Open your book and read.
5.	Close your book and write.	Open your book and repeat.
6.	Close your book and repeat.	Open your book and read.

TASK 8

Listen and match.

1. Listen   a. book and write.
2. Close your   b. your book and repeat.
3. Listen and   c. and point.
4. Close   d. and match.
5. Open   e. circle.
6. Listen   f. your book and read.

TASK 9

Listen and write.

1. Listen _____ point.
2. _____ and _____.
3. _____ write.
4. _____ your _____.
5. Listen _____.
6. _____.

TASK 10

Listen and write, then match.

1. _____

2. _____

3. _____

4. _____

5. _____

6. _____

7. _____

8. _____

9. _____

10. _____

Pair Work: Student A

1. Read to Student B:

a. Circle.

b. Write.

c. Read.

d. Listen.

e. Match.

f. Point.

g. Listen and point.

h. Don't write.

i. Listen and match.

j. Read and write.

k. Listen and circle.

l. Open your book.

2. Repeat.

3. Read to Student B:

a. Read.

b. Write.

c. Ask.

d. Answer.

e. Point.

f. Circle

g. Listen and match.

h. Ask and answer.

i. Listen. Don't write.

j. Point and repeat.

k. Close your book.

l. Listen and circle.

4. Write.

Pair Work: Student B

1. Repeat.

2. Read to Student A:

a. Match.

b. Write.

c. Read.

d. Circle.

e. Point.

f. Listen.

g. Don't write.

h. Don't read.

i. Listen and point.

j. Ask and answer.

k. Listen and circle.

l. Repeat and write.

3. Write.

4. Read to Student A:

a. Point.

b. Repeat.

c. Answer.

d. Circle.

e. Ask.

f. Read.

g. Read and write.

h. Listen and repeat.

i. Read and match.

j. Don't write.

k. Listen and circle.

l. Point and repeat.

2

Ask and answer.

Getting Ready

Listen and point.

Listen and repeat.

TASK 1

Listen and point. Listen and repeat.

AB	CD	EF	GH	IJ
KL	MN	OP	QR	ST
	UV	WX	YZ	

TASK 2

Listen and point. Listen and circle.

	A	*B*	*C*	*D*
1.	A	(B)	C	D
2.	E	F	G	H
3.	I	J	K	L
4.	M	N	O	P
5.	Q	R	S	T
6.	U	V	W	
7.	X	Y	Z	

TASK 3

Listen and circle or don't circle.

Circle A.   Don't circle B.   Circle C.   Don't circle D.

	A	*B*	*C*	*D*
1.	(A)	B	(C)	D
2.	E	F	G	H
3.	I	J	K	L
4.	M	N	O	P
5.	Q	R	S	T
6.	U	V	W	
7.	X	Y	Z	

TASK 4

Listen and circle.

	A	B	C
1.	AB	(DD)	BH
2.	CD	VB	DE
3.	FG	DG	BG
4.	HI	HJ	HK
5.	KL	AL	KA
6.	MN	MM	NN

TASK 5

Questions and answers. Listen and repeat.

		Question	*Answer*
1.	ABC	[eɪ bi si]	[yɛs eɪ bi si]
		ABC?	Yes, ABC.
		DEF?	Yes, DEF.
2.	GHI	[dʒi eɪtʃ aɪ]	[no dʒeɪ keɪ ɛl]
		GHI?	No, JKL.
		MNO?	No, PQR.
3.	STU or VWX?	[ɛs ti uy	[vi dəbəlyu ɛks]
		vi dəbəlyu ɛks]	
		STU or VWX?	VWX.
		UVW or XYZ?	XYZ.

TASK 6

Listen and circle.

	A	B	C
1.	yes	no	(or)
2.	yes	no	or
3.	yes	no	or
4.	yes	no	or
5.	yes	no	or

TASK 7

Listen and circle.

ABC	DEF	GHI
JKL	MNO	PQR
STU	VW	XYZ

TASK 8

Listen and match.

1. AB	CD
2. EF	GH
3. IJ	KL
4. MN	OP
5. QR	ST
6. UV	WX

TASK 9

Listen and write.

A: Write _____.   A: No, _____.

B: _____?   B: _____?

                                  A: Yes, _____.

TASK 10

Listen and write.

A: Write _____.   A: No, _____.

B: _____.   B: _____?

A: No, _____.   A: Yes, _____.

B: _____?

Pair Work: Student A

1. **Student A: Read.**

    Student B: Point.

    Student A: Answer Yes or No.

AB	CD	EF	GH	IJ
KL	MN	OP	QR	ST
	UV	WX	YZ	

2. **Student A: Read.**

    Student B: Close your book and write.

BF	CZ	YM	OL	PY	TG
LE	QS	NW	RU	AK	DE

Pair Work: Student B

1. **Student B: Read.**

    Student A: Point.

    Student B: Answer Yes or No.

QR	MN	IJ	EF	WX
KL	YZ	AB	UV	OP
	CD	GH	ST	

2. **Student A: Read.**

    Student B: Close your book and write.

TH	PF	XN	MB	RY	WO
JL	AV	CS	GE	KI	QN

3

Capital A, small c.

Getting Ready

Listen and point.

Listen and repeat.

TASK 1

Listen and check, circle, or underline.

CAPITAL LETTERS	A ✔	B	C	D	E̲	F	G	H	I	J
small letters	a	b	ⓒ	d	e	f	g	h	i	j

TASK 2

Listen and circle.

Ⓚ	L	M	N
T	CAPITAL		O
S	R	Q	P

k	l	m	n
t	small		o
s	r	q	ⓟ

TASK 3

Listen and check or underline.

U ✔	V	W	X	Y	Z
u	y̲	w	x	y	z

TASK 4

Listen and circle or underline.

A a	B b	C c	D d	E e	F f	G g
H h	I i	J j	K k	L l	M m	N n
O o	P p	Q q	R r	S̲ s	T t	U u
V v	W ⓦ	X x	Y y	Z z		

Game

Match the capital and the small letters.

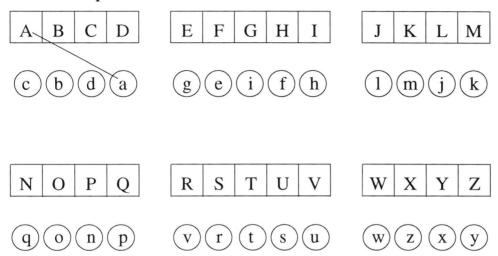

TASK 5

Slow and fast speech. Listen and repeat.

	Slow	*Fast*
1. letters	[lɛtɚz]	[lɛdɚz]
	letters	letters
	Check the letters.	
	Circle the letters.	
	Underline the letters.	
2. capital	[kæpɪtəl]	[kæpədl]
	capital	capital
	Check the capital letters.	
	Circle the capital letters.	
	Underline the capital letters.	
3. small	[smɔl]	[smɔl]
	small	small
	Check the small letters.	
	Circle the small letters.	
	Underline the small letters.	

TASK 6

Listen and check.

	CAPITAL LETTERS					small letters				
1.	A ✔	F	H	J	K	a	f	h	j	k
2.	X	G	H	G	V	x	g	h ✔	g	v
3.	P	T	U	V	C	p	t	u	v	c
4.	S	L	F	H	X	s	l	f	h	x
5.	D	V	B	G	C	d	v	b	g	c
6.	N	E	M	O	U	n	e	m	o	u
7.	L	W	R	Q	U	l	w	r	q	u
8.	A	J	K	I	Y	a	j	k	i	y

TASK 7

Listen and write.

1.	___ ___	6.	___ ___ ___
2.	___ ___	7.	___ ___ ___
3.	___ ___	8.	___ ___ ___ ___
4.	___ ___ ___	9.	___ ___ ___ ___
5.	___ ___ ___	10.	___ ___ ___ ___

TASK 8

Listen and check.

1.	circle	check	underline
2.	write	circle	check
3.	underline	circle	write
4.	small a	capital K	small f
5.	small letters	capital letters	capital W

TASK 9

Listen and write.

1. _____ the _____.
2. _____ the _____.
3. _____ the _____.
4. _____.
5. _____.
6. _____.
7. _____.

TASK 10

Listen and write.

1. _____ the _____.
2. _____ the _____.
3. _____.
4. _____.
5. _____.
6. _____ and _____.
7. _____.

Pair Work: Student A

1. **Student A: Read.**

   Student B: Point.

   Student A: Answer Yes or No.

a	E	B	c	A	f
C	b	F	e	D	d

2. **Student A: Read**

   Student B: Close your book and write.

yP	GH	iL	JM	nm	xC
zO	Kq	rW	qu	sV	Tf

Pair Work: Student B

1. **Student B: Read.**

   Student A: Point.

   Student B: Answer Yes or No.

H	i	G	h	L	I
K	j	k	g	I	J

2. **Student B: Read.**

   Student A: Close your book and write.

mM	Af	Ot	ce	pv	Qx
us	Ry	wb	Gi	hD	Nz

4

Fill in the blanks.

Getting Ready

Listen and point.

Listen and repeat.

TASK 1

Listen and point. Listen and repeat.

1	2	3
4	5	6
7	8	9

TASK 2

Listen and point. Listen and circle or don't circle.

1 one	2 two	③ three
4 four	5 five	6 six
7 seven	8 eight	9 nine

TASK 3

Listen and circle.

	X	Y	Z
a.	4	②	3
b.	5	6	1
c.	7	9	1
d.	8	6	5
e.	5	4	9
f.	2	8	7

TASK 4

Listen and circle.

	X	Y	Z
a.	(six)	eight	seven
b.	one	nine	five
c.	seven	four	three
d.	two	six	four
e.	three	two	five
f.	eight	one	seven

Matching Game

Match the words and numbers.   **Fill in the blanks.**

Words	Numbers
one	3
five	6
seven	5
six	1
three	2
eight	9
two	4
nine	8
four	7

o _n_ e   s i __

t w __   s e __ e __

t __ r __ e   e i __ __ t

f __ u r   n __ __ e

f __ v __

TASK 5

Slow and fast speech. Listen and repeat.

		Slow	Fast
1.	in the	[ɪ n ðə]	[ɪ n:ə]
		in the	in the
		Fill in the blanks.	Fill in the blanks.
2.	write the	[raɪt ðə]	[raɪtðə]
		write the	write the
		Write the words.	Write the words.

3. listen and

[lɪsɛn ɛnd]   [lɪsɛnən]

listen and   lis'n 'n

Listen and write.   Listen and write.

Listen and read.   Listen and read.

Listen and ask.   Listen and ask.

Listen and answer.   Listen and answer.

TASK 6

Listen and write the words.

a. _____   f. _____

b. _____   g. _____

c. _____   h. _____

d. _____   i. _____

e. _____   j. _____

TASK 7

Listen and write the numbers.

a. _____3_____   f. _____   k. _____

b. _____   g. _____   l. _____

c. _____   h. _____   m. _____

d. _____   i. _____   n. _____

e. _____   j. _____   o. _____

TASK 8

Listen and fill in the blanks.

a. 7 4 <u>1</u> 9   f. 3 __ 6 __

b. 3 8 5 __   g. 7 __ __ 9

c. 2 9 __ __   h. 6 __ __ __

d. 6 4 __ __   i. __ 2 __ __

e. __ 3 __ 4   j. __ __ 4 __

TASK 9

Listen and fill in the blanks.

A: _____ the word _____.

B: _____?

A: Yes, and _____ the number _____.

B: _____.

A: No, _____.

B: _____?

A: _____.

TASK 10

Listen and fill in the blanks.

1.   _____ the number _____.

2.   _____ the word _____.

3.   Write _____.

4.   _____ seven.

5.   _____.

6.   _____.

7.   _____.

Pair Work: Student A

1. Read to Student B.

seven	one	eight	five	two
six	three	nine	one	four

2. Listen and write the words.

3. Read to Student B.

3	1	7	9	5	6
85	49	21	33	76	68
719	917	728	635	294	851

4. Listen and write the numbers.

Pair Work: Student B

1. **Listen and write the words.**

2. **Read to Student A.**

nine	one	one	eight	four
seven	three	two	six	five

3. **Listen and write the numbers.**

4. **Read to Student A.**

4	3	8	2	8	1
55	64	37	82	19	98
191	283	476	518	918	598

5

First point. Then repeat.

Getting Ready

First listen. Then listen and repeat.

① First dictate to Student C.

You   Your Partner   Student C   Student D

② Second dictate to Student D.

You   Your Partner   Student C   Student D

③ Third dictate to your partner.

You   Your Partner   Student C   Student D

④ Now dictate to your partner again.

You   Your Partner   Student C   Student D

TASK 1

Now listen and point. Then listen and point again. Last listen and repeat.

 Student C

 Your Partner

 Student D

Numbers	Words	Numbers	Words
1	one	1st	first
2	two	2nd	second
3	three	3rd	third

TASK 2

First listen and point. Then listen and repeat.

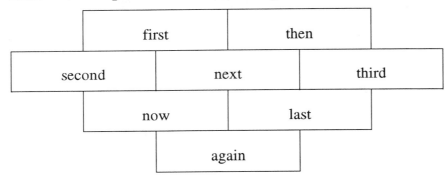

TASK 3

First listen and point. Then listen and circle.

	A	B	C
1.	(first)	second	third
2.	first	next	last
3.	next	now	again
4.	first	next	third
5.	first	second	last
6.	now	next	again
7.	first	next	then
8.	next	then	again
9.	first	now	last

TASK 4

Listen and circle.

	A	B	C
1.	dictate	(read)	write
2.	dictate	circle	point
3.	close	circle	don't
4.	repeat	match	open
5.	ask	answer	read
6.	read	dictate	ask
7.	write	read	match

Matching Game

Match the words and numbers.

Numbers	Words	Numbers	Words
1	two	4th	third
2	three	1st	fourth
3	one	3rd	second
4	four	2nd	first

TASK 5

Slow and fast speech. First listen. Then listen and repeat.

		Slow	Fast
1.	first	[fɚst]	[fɚs]
		first	first
		First read.	First read.
		First write.	First write.
2.	second	[sɛkənd]	[sɛkn]
		second	second
		Second write the words.	Second write the words.
		Second dictate.	Second dictate.

3. third   [θɚd] [æsk]   [θɚdæsk]
                            third ask   third ask
                            Third ask.   Third ask.
                            Third answer.   Third answer.

4. next   [nɛkst]   [nɛks]
                            next   next
                            Next listen.   Next listen.
                            Next dictate.   Next dictate.

5. last   [læst]   [læs]
                            last   last
                            Last read.   Last read.
                            Last match.   Last match.

TASK 6

First listen and point. Then listen and match. Then listen and point again.

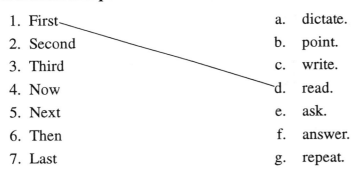

1. First   a.   dictate.
2. Second   b.   point.
3. Third   c.   write.
4. Now   d.   read.
5. Next   e.   ask.
6. Then   f.   answer.
7. Last   g.   repeat.

TASK 7

Listen and write the words.

Keywords

| book | partner |
| words | numbers |

1. Circle the _____.
2. Read to your _____.
3. Answer your _____.
4. Write the _____.

5. Ask your _____.

6. Write the _____.

7. Close your _____.

8. Dictate to your _____.

9. Open your _____.

TASK 8

First listen. Then listen and point. Then listen again and write the numbers.

circle	match	repeat
____	____	____
read	dictate	write
____	____	____
ask	answer	point
____	____	____
listen	open	close
____	_1_	_12_

TASK 9

First listen. Then listen and fill in the blanks.

1. _____ listen.

2. _____ listen and repeat.

3. _____ listen and point.

4. _____ listen and _____.

5. _____ listen and _____.

6. _____ listen _____.

7. _____.

TASK 10

First listen. Then listen and fill in the blanks.

1. First _____ your _____.
2. Second _____ the _____.
3. Next, _____.
4. Now, _____.
5. Then, _____.
6. _____.
7. _____.

Pair Work: Student A

1. Dictate to your partner.

first	next	last	now	then
second	then	again	third	next

2. First close your book. Then listen to your partner and write the words.

3. Dictate to your partner.

9	6	5	1	3	7
805	49	12	48	67	55
709	907	143	413	722	484

4. First close your book. Then listen to your partner and write the numbers.

Pair Work: Student B

1. First close your book. Then listen to your partner and write the words.

2. Dictate to your partner.

last	second	third	first	now
then	then	again	next	again

3. First close your book. Then listen to your partner and write the numbers.

4. Dictate to your partner.

1	3	4	6	7	8
558	129	763	198	607	344
72	90	43	13	72	84

6

Line 2, column B.

Getting Ready

First listen and point. Then listen and repeat.

	Column A	Column B	Column C
Line 1	9	10	11
Line 2	12	13	14
Line 3	15	16	17

TASK 1

First listen and point. Then listen and circle or don't circle.

	Column A	Column B	Column C	Column D	Column E	Column F	Column G	Column H	Column I	Column J
Line 1	⓪	1	2	3	4	5	6	7	8	9
Line 2	10	11	12	13	14	15	16	17	18	19

TASK 2

Listen and circle the number or the word.

Number	0	①	2	3	4
Word	zero	one	two	three	four
Number	5	6	7	8	9
Word	five	six	seven	eight	nine
Number	10	11	12	13	14
Word	ten	eleven	twelve	thirteen	fourteen
Number	15	16	17	18	19
Word	fifteen	sixteen	seventeen	eighteen	nineteen

TASK 3

Listen and circle.

	X	Y	Z
a.	3	⑬	16
b.	15	5	9
c.	4	12	10
d.	11	9	7
e.	17	2	12
f.	14	16	5
g.	9	19	5
h.	18	16	7
i.	7	5	16
j.	17	7	11

TASK 4

Listen and circle.

X	Y	Z
a. zero	eleven	(thirteen)
b. twelve	nineteen	fourteen
c. fifteen	sixteen	thirteen
d. seventeen	twelve	ten
e. ten	zero	twelve
f. nineteen	eighteen	fourteen
g. eighteen	sixteen	thirteen
h. eleven	twelve	seventeen
i. zero	ten	twelve
j. fourteen	fifteen	sixteen
k. eleven	thirteen	seventeen

TASK 5

Slow and fast speech. First listen. Then listen and repeat.

		Slow	*Fast*
1. what is		[wət] [ɪz]	[wəts]
		what is	what's
		What is line 2, column B?	What's line 2, column B?
		What is line 4, column C?	What's line 4, column C?
2. it is		[ɪt] [ɪz]	[ɪts]
		it is	it's
		It is 13. (*thirteen*)	It's 13. (*thirteen*)
		It is 11. (*eleven*)	It's 11. (*eleven*)

TASK 6

First listen and fill in the blanks. Then match the numbers and words.

Column 1	Column 2
Numbers	*Words*
a. _11_	nineteen
b. ___	___
c. ___	___
d. ___	___
e. ___	___
f. ___	___
g. ___	___
h. ___	___
i. ___	___
j. ___	___

TASK 7

First listen and point. Then listen and circle or don't circle.

Column 1	Column 2	Column 3	Column 4	Column 5
(What's)	What's	What's	What's	What's
It's	It's	It's	It's	It's

TASK 8

Listen and circle.

	Column A	Column B	Column C	Column D
Line 1	0	1	2	3
Line 2	4	⑤	6	7
Line 3	8	9	10	11
Line 4	12	13	14	15
Line 5	16	17	18	19

TASK 9

First listen. Then listen and fill in the blanks.

A: _____ line _____, column _____?

B: It's _____.

A: What's _____, column_____?

B: _____.

A: _____?

B: No, _____.

A: _____.

B: Yes, and _____?

A: _____.

TASK 10

First listen. Then listen and fill in the blanks. Write the words.

	Column A	Column B	Column C
Line 1			
Line 2	thirteen		
Line 3		fourteen	

Pair Work: Student A

1. **Dictate to your partner.**

Write the number 17.   Write the word eight.

7	nine	thirteen	0	19
eighteen	12	ten	11	fourteen
16	11	9	twelve	six

2. **First close your book. Then listen to your partner and write the words or numbers.**

3. **Ask your partner:** *What's line _____, Column _____?*

	Column A	Column B	Column C	Column D
Line 1				
Line 2				
Line 3				

4. **Answer your partner.**

	Column A	Column B	Column C	Column D
Line 1	13	0	19	12
Line 2	10	15	9	16
Line 3	14	18	17	11

Pair Work: Student B

1. **First close your book. Then listen to your partner and write the words or numbers.**

2. **Dictate to your partner.**

Write the number 11.   Write the word thirteen.

0	twelve	19	eighteen	thirteen
10	9	sixteen	seventeen	14
13	19	fifteen	16	17

3. Answer your partner.

	Column A	Column B	Column C	Column D
Line 1	16	0	15	11
Line 2	12	17	14	7
Line 3	19	10	18	13

4. Ask your partner. *What's line _____, Column ____?*

	Column A	Column B	Column C	Column D
Line 1				
Line 2				
Line 3				

7

Check the answers.

First listen and point. Then listen and repeat.

| Yes | = | Right | No | = | Wrong |

TASK 1

First listen and point. Then listen and repeat.

E5	A19	D6
B13	C11	C12

TASK 2

First listen and point. Then listen and match.

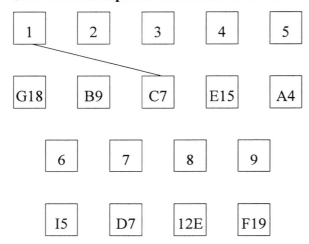

TASK 3

First listen and point. Then listen and circle.

	A	B	C	D
1.	(right)	wrong	yes	no
2.	right	wrong	yes	no
3.	right	wrong	yes	no
4.	right	wrong	yes	no
5.	right	wrong	yes	no
6.	right	wrong	yes	no

TASK 4

Listen and circle.

	Answers		Questions	
1.	check	dictate	(check)	dictate
2.	circle	answer	circle	answer
3.	write	read	write	read
4.	read	repeat	read	repeat
5.	read	point to	read	point to
6.	circle	ask	circle	ask
7.	read	write	read	write
8.	match	point to	match	point to
9.	dictate	write	dictate	write

TASK 5

Singular and plural speech. First listen. Then listen and repeat.

		One	*Two or more*
1. question		[kwɛstʃən]	[kwɛstʃənz]
		question	questions
		Read the question.	Read the questions.
		Answer the question.	Answer the questions.
2. answer		[ænsɚ]	[ænsɚz]
		answer	answers
		Read the answer.	Read the answers.
		Write the answer.	Write the answers.

TASK 6

Listen and circle.

	A	B	C	D
1.	question	questions	answer	(answers)
2.	question	questions	answer	answers
3.	question	questions	answer	answers
4.	question	questions	answer	answers
5.	question	questions	answer	answers
6.	question	questions	answer	answers
7.	question	questions	answer	answers
8.	question	questions	answer	answers
9.	question	questions	answer	answers

TASK 7

Listen and fill in the blanks.

F8 _____	K9 _____	B9 wrong	R5 _____	A17 _____
H17 right	N6 _____	M2 _____	L14 _____	X18 _____

Game

Fill in the blanks.

1	2	3	4	5
one	_____	three	four	five
1st	2nd	3rd	_____	_____
first	second	_____	fourth	fifth

6	7	8	9	10
_____	_____	_____	_____	_____
____th	____th	_____	_____	____th
_____	_____	eighth	ninth	_____

TASK 8

Listen and mark the answers right or wrong.

✓ = right	1 ✓	2 ____	3 ____	4 ____	5 ____
✗ = wrong	6 ____	7 ____	8 ✗	9 ____	10 ____

TASK 9

Listen and write the number.

A14	D5	D12	D9
1	____	____	____
C11	B12	E11	B18
____	____	____	____
E18	C9	A13	C7
____	____	2	____

TASK 10

First listen. Then listen again and fill in the blanks.

A: What's _____ to _____ question?

B: _____ question?

A: _____ question.

B: _____ .

A: _____ ?

B: _____ .

A: Thank you. And what's _____ to _____ ?

B: _____ to _____ is _____ .

Pair Work: Student A

1. **First dictate the letters and numbers to your partner. Then check the answers.**

   A14   B10   D9   F11   H7   C12

   E17   H6   A18   B4   C16   D5

2. **Listen to your partner and write the numbers and letters.**

3. **First listen to your partner and answer the questions. Then check the answers.**

	A	B	C
1	Z5	V13	X12
2	U2	R11	T4
3	W7	Y10	S16

4. **First ask your partner. Then write the answers.**

	X	Y	Z
10			
11			
12			

Pair Work: Student B

1. **Listen to your partner and write the letters and numbers.**

2. **First dictate the numbers and letters to your partner. Then check the answers.**

   19Z   2R   14Q   7N   17P   4Y
   6S   11M   15J   9Q   7T   13U

3. **First ask your partner. Then write the answers.**

	A	B	C
1			
2			
3			

4. **First listen to your partner and answer the questions. Then check the answers.**

	X	Y	Z
10	12C	9B	11D
11	5A	6G	10E
12	19G	13F	16H

8

Turn to page 23.

Getting Ready

First listen and point. Then listen and repeat.

TASK 1

First listen and point. Then listen and repeat.

TASK 2

First listen and point. Then listen and check or underline.

20	30	40	50
60	70 ✓	80	90

TASK 3

First listen and point. Then listen and underline.

	A	B	C	D
1.	20	30	<u>40</u>	50
2.	60	70	80	90
3.	20	30	40	50
4.	60	70	80	90
5.	20	30	40	50
6.	60	70	80	90
7.	20	30	40	50
8.	60	70	80	90

TASK 4

Listen and circle.

	A	B	C
1.	(twenty)	forty	sixty
2.	seventy	fifty	sixty
3.	thirty	sixty	forty
4.	eighty	thirty	ninety
5.	fifty	ninety	sixty
6.	twenty	seventy	thirty
7.	sixty	thirty	eighty
8.	forty	seventy	twenty

Matching Game

Match the words and numbers.

20	thirty	60	eighty
30	fifty	70	ninety
40	twenty	80	seventy
50	forty	90	sixty

TASK 5

Slow and fast speech. First listen. Then listen and repeat.

		Slow	*Fast*
1.	20	[twɛnti]	[twɛni]
2.	30	[θɚti]	[θɚdi]
3.	40	[fɔɚti]	[fɔɚdi]
4.	50	[fɪfti]	[fɪfdi]
5.	60	[sɪksti]	[sɪksdi]
6.	70	[sɛvɛnti]	[sɛvəndi]
7.	80	[eɪti]	[eɪdi]
8.	90	[naɪnti]	[naɪndi]

TASK 6

Listen and circle.

Turn to page ____:	5	(14)	27	38	47	59	64	73	85	96
Turn back to page ____:	5	14	27	38	47	59	64	73	85	96
Turn to page ____ again:	5	14	27	38	47	59	64	73	85	96
Show me page ____:	5	14	27	38	47	59	64	73	85	96
Show me page ____ again:	5	14	27	38	47	59	64	73	85	96

TASK 7

Listen and circle.

	A	B	C
1.	(21)	77	71
2.	23	34	54
3.	57	97	67
4.	59	95	99
5.	22	27	72
6.	21	25	29
7.	83	73	53
8.	56	55	65
9.	38	48	58
10.	59	51	55

TASK 8

First listen and match. Then mark right or wrong.

Order	Answer	Right=✔ Wrong=✗	Answer	Right=✔ Wrong=✗
First	37	____	45	____
Second	63	____	28	____
Third	94	____	72	✗
Fourth	56	____	29	____
Fifth	81	✔	38	____
Sixth	57	____	92	____
Seventh	83	____	61	____
Eighth	46	____	74	____

TASK 9

Listen and fill in the blanks.

A: Turn to _____.

B: _____?

A: _____.

B: Right, _____.

A: What's _____?

B: It's _____.

A: Right. And _____?

B: D14.

A: What's the answer to the fifth question?

B: _____.

A: _____. It's _____.

TASK 10

Listen and fill in the blanks.

A: First, _____.

B: _____.

A: _____ me the _____.

B: Here. _____.

A: _____. What's _____?

B: _____.

A: Right. Now _____. Show _____.

B: _____.

Pair Work: Student A

1. Dictate to your partner. Then check the answers.

Turn to page ____:	7	11	24	33	40	57	69	76	82	95
Turn back to page ____:	7	11	24	33	40	57	69	76	82	95
Turn to page ____ again:	7	11	24	33	40	57	69	76	82	95
Show me page ____:	7	11	24	33	40	57	69	76	82	95
Show me page ____ again:	7	11	24	33	40	57	69	76	82	95

2. Listen to your partner and write. Then show your answers to your partner.

Turn to page ____:										
Turn back to page ____:										
Turn to page ____ again:										
Show me page ____:										
Show me page ____ again:										

3. **First ask your partner to turn to the right page. Then ask your partner to show you the page.**

12	24	96	48	72
68	36	27	39	83
56	91	22	94	17

4. **First listen to your partner and turn to the right page. Then show your partner the page.**

Pair Work: Student B

1. **Listen to your partner and write. Then show your answers to your partner.**

Turn to page ____:										
Turn back to page ____:										
Turn to page ____ again:										
Show me page ____:										
Show me page ____ again:										

2. **Dictate to your partner. Then check the answers.**

Turn to page ____:	4	17	26	32	49	58	66	75	87	93
Turn back to page ____:	4	17	26	32	49	58	66	75	87	93
Turn to page ____ again:	4	17	26	32	49	58	66	75	87	93
Show me page ____:	4	17	26	32	49	58	66	75	87	93
Show me page ____ again:	4	17	26	32	49	58	66	75	87	93

3. **First listen to your partner and turn to the right page. Then show your partner the page.**

4. **First ask your partner to turn to the right page. Then ask your partner to show you the page.**

56	43	82	94	44
39	82	75	61	50
72	27	69	37	77

9

B as in Boston.

Getting Ready

First listen and point. Then listen and repeat.

TASK 1

First listen and point. Then listen and repeat.

TASK 2

First listen and point. Then listen and check.

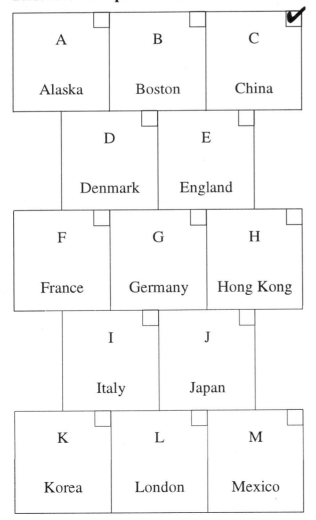

TASK 3

First listen and point to the word. Then listen and write the letter.

<u>N</u> as in New York   ____ as in Spain   ____ as in Washington

____ as in Ohio   ____ as in Tokyo   ____ as in X-ray

____ as in Paris   ____ as in Uruguay   ____ as in Yemen

____ as in Quebec   ____ as in Vietnam   ____ as in Zambia

____ as in Rome

TASK 4

Listen and underline the letter or word.

A Alaska	B Boston	C China	<u>D</u> Denmark
E England	F France	G Germany	H Hong Kong
I Italy	J Japan	K Korea	L London
M Mexico	N New York	O Ohio	P Paris
Q Quebec	R Rome	S Spain	T Tokyo
U Urugay	V Vietnam	W Washington	X X-ray
Y Yemen	Z Zambia		

TASK 5

Slow and fast speech. First listen. Then listen and repeat.

	Slow	*Fast*
1. as in	[æzɪn]	[æzn]
	as in	as'n
	as in Denmark	as 'n Denmark
2. how do you	[haʊ du yu]	[haʊdəyə]
	how do you	how do you
	How do you spell that?	How do you spell that?
3. spell that	[spɛl ðæt]	[spɛlət']
	spell that	spell that
	How do you spell that?	How do you spell that?

4.   word   [wɚd]   [wɚd']
                                        word   word
                                        the right word   the right word
                                        the first word   the first word
                                        the second word   the second word

TASK 6

First listen and fill in the blanks. Then match the letters and the words.

Letter	As In	Letter	As in
F	New York	___	Mexico
___	Denmark	___	Spain
___	Vietnam	___	Germany
___	France	___	Zambia
___	China	___	Boston

TASK 7

Listen and circle.

	A	B	C
1.	CAnada	GERmany	MExico
2.	WAshington	Uruguay	Italy
3.	OHIo	KoREa	ALAska
4.	BOston	DEnmark	TOkyo
5.	HOng KOng	X-ray	ENgland
6.	LOndon	PAris	VIEtnam
7.	JaPAn	New YORk	QueBEc
8.	FRAnce	SPAIn	ROme

TASK 8

Listen and fill in the blanks.

A: C _____-A-R-O-L-I-_____-A.

B: _____ the first word?

A: _____ the _____ letter _____?

B: _____.

A: How do you spell _____ word?

B: G _____-E-O-R-G-_____-I-_____.

A: G-E-O-R-_____.

B: _____.

TASK 9

Listen and fill in the blanks.

A: What's _____ letter?

B: _____.

A: _____?

B: No, _____. _____ as in _____.

A: Right, _____. And what's the _____?

B: _____.

TASK 10

Listen and fill in the blanks.

A: How _____?

B: S-U-_____-A.

A: What's _____?

B: _____.

A: _____?

B: No, _____.

A: _____.

Pair Work: Student A

1. **First circle ten words. Then read the words to your partner.**

ALAska	HOngKong	OHIo	VIEtnam
BOston	Italy	PAris	WAshington
CAnada	JaPAn	QueBEc	X-ray
DEnmark	KoREa	ROme	YEmen
ENgland	LOndon	SPAIn	ZAmbia
FRAnce	MExico	TOkyo	
GERmany	New YORk	URuguay	

2. **Listen to your partner and spell the words.**

3. **First spell the words for your partner. Then check the answers.**

Arkansas	Oaxaca	Zonguldak	Djibouti
Manaus	Ningxia	Kawasaki	Vanuatu

4. **First listen to your partner and write the words. Then show your partner the answers.**

Pair Work: Student B

1. **Listen to your partner and spell the words.**

2. **First circle ten words. Then read the words to your partner.**

ALAska	HOngKong	OHIo	VIEtnam
BOston	Italy	PAris	WAshington
CAnada	JaPAn	QueBEc	X-ray
DEnmark	KoREa	ROme	YEmen
ENgland	LOndon	SPAIn	ZAmbia
FRAnce	MExico	TOkyo	
GERmany	New YORk	URuguay	

3. **First listen to your partner and write the words. Then show your partner the answers.**

4. **First spell the words for your partner. Then check the answers.**

Reykjavik	Dnepropetrovsk	Qinghai	Tuxtla
Antananarivo	Muang Phrae	Bilbao	Xochimilco

10

Write the order.

Getting Ready

First listen and point. Then listen and repeat.

TASK 1

First listen and point. Then listen and repeat.

DBAC	ZXWY	EGFH	QPOR	STUV	KIJ	NML

TASK 2

What's the order? Listen and check the right answers.

	☑		
1	XYZ	ZYX	XZY
2	HIJ	JIH	IJH
3	MNL	NML	NLM
4	OPR	PRU	RYP
5	OGG	OCG	OGC
6	PTT	TPP	PPT
7	TSV	VST	STV
8	BDB	BGD	DGZ

TASK 3

Listen and match.

Order   Picture Number

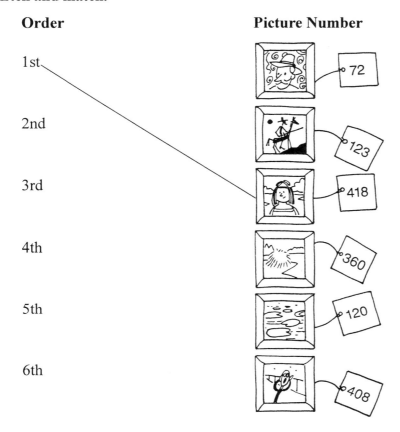

1st

2nd

3rd

4th

5th

6th

72

123

418

360

120

408

TASK 4

Listen and write the order.

_____ B	_____ 7	_____ N
_____ S	__1__ 18	_____ y

TASK 5

Slow and fast speech. First listen. Then listen and repeat.

	Slow	*Fast*
1. the	[ðə]	[ðə]
	the	the
	the words	the words
	the questions	the questions
2. the	[ðə]	[ði]
	the	the
	the order	the order
	the answers	the answers
3. look at	[lʊk æt]	[lʊkəd']
	look at	look at
	Look at the words.	Look at the words.
	Look at the order.	Look at the order.
4. your partner	[yuɚ paɚtnɚ]	[yɚ paɚtnɚ]
	your partner	your partner
	Ask your partner.	Ask your partner.
	Tell your partner.	Tell your partner.

TASK 6

Listen and check the right answers.

	Ask your partner		Tell your partner	
1.	the answers	the order	the answers	the order
2.	the questions	the order	the questions	the order
3.	the question	the questions	the question	the questions
4.	the answer	the answers	the answer	the answers
5.	the number	the answer	the number	the answer
6.	the answer	the answers	the answer	the answers

TASK 7

Look, listen, and write the order.

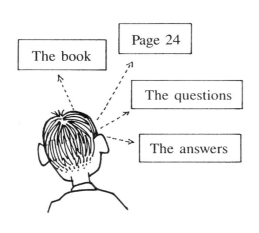

_____	___1___
the order	the words
_____	_____
the questions	the answers
_____	_____
page 48	the letters
_____	_____
page 24	the numbers

TASK 8

Listen and circle.

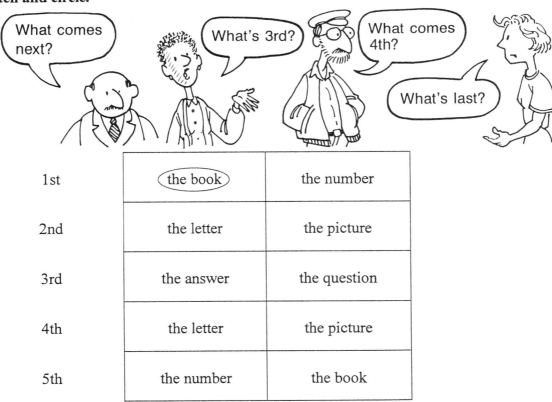

1st	the book	the number
2nd	the letter	the picture
3rd	the answer	the question
4th	the letter	the picture
5th	the number	the book

TASK 9

Listen and fill in the blanks.

A: What _____?

B: Capital _____.

A: Capital _____?

B: No, _____. _____ as in _____ and _____ as in _____.

A: And _____?

B: _____.

A: Capital _____.

B: _____.

TASK 10

Listen and fill in the blanks.

A: _____?

B: _____.

A: _____?

B: No, _____. _____ as in _____.

A: What comes next?

B: _____. _____ as in _____, _____ as in _____,

_____ as in _____.

A: _____.

B: _____.

Pair Work: Student A

1. First listen to your partner and answer the questions. Then check the answers.

	A	B	C	D	E
	A	*B*	*C*	*D*	*E*
1.	1st	7th	8th	3rd	10th
2.	17th	2nd	13th	18th	4th
3.	6th	19th	5th	14th	11th
4.	12th	9th	20th	16th	15th

2. First ask your partner the order. Then fill in the answers. Last show your partner the answers.

	A	B	C	D	E
1.					
2.					
3.					
4.					

Pair Work: Student B

1. First ask your partner the order. Then fill in the answers. Last show your partner the answers.

	A	B	C	D	E
1.					
2.					
3.					
4.					

2. First listen to your partner and answer the questions. Then check the answers.

	A	B	C	D	E
1.	4th	8th	19th	14th	6th
2.	13th	9th	1st	2nd	15th
3.	17th	3rd	20th	18th	11th
4.	7th	12th	10th	5th	16th

11

A pen and two pieces of paper.

Getting Ready

First listen and point. Then listen and repeat.

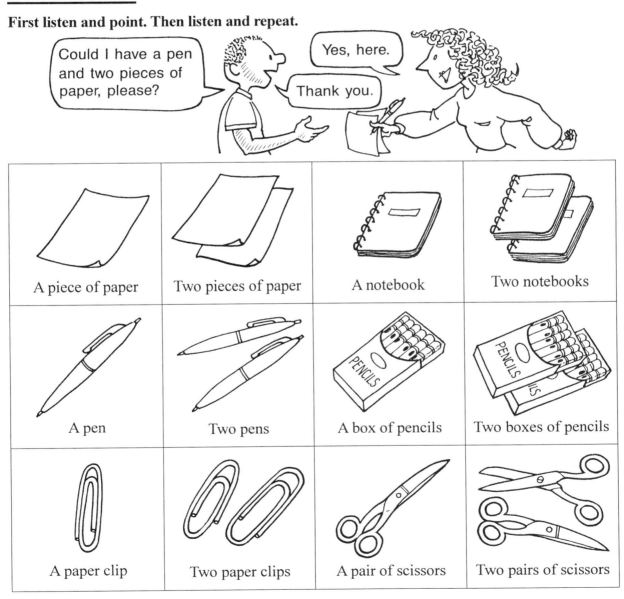

A piece of paper	Two pieces of paper	A notebook	Two notebooks
A pen	Two pens	A box of pencils	Two boxes of pencils
A paper clip	Two paper clips	A pair of scissors	Two pairs of scissors

TASK 1

Look at the pictures again, listen, and point. Then ask and answer the questions with your partner.

TASK 2

Listen and write the order.

_____	a pair of scissors
_____	two notebooks and a paper clip
_____	a piece of paper and a paper clip
_____	two pens
_____	two boxes of pencils and a pair of scissors
_____	a box of pencils, two paper clips, and two pieces of paper
_____	a paper clip and a pen
___1___	a box of pencils

TASK 3

Listen and match.

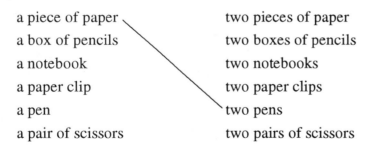

a piece of paper   two pieces of paper

a box of pencils   two boxes of pencils

a notebook   two notebooks

a paper clip   two paper clips

a pen   two pens

a pair of scissors   two pairs of scissors

TASK 4

Listen and write the order.

1. _a notebook_   4. _____
2. _____   5. _____
3. _____   6. _____

TASK 5

Singular and plural speech. First listen. Then listen and repeat.

Singular	*Plural*
1.	[əz]
piece	pieces
box	boxes
a piece of paper	two pieces of paper
a box of pencils	two boxes of pencils
a box of paper clips	two boxes of paper clips
2.	[s]
notebook	notebooks
paper clip	paper clips
Could I have a notebook?	Could I have two notebooks?
Could I have a paper clip?	Could I have two paper clips?
3.	[z]
pen	pens
pencil	pencils
pair	pairs
Could I have a pen?	Could I have two pens?
Could I have a pencil?	Could I have two pencils?
a pair of scissors	two pairs of scissors

TASK 6

Listen and write the order.

_____	a piece of paper	___1___	a paper clip
_____	two pieces of paper	_____	two paper clips
_____	a box of pencils	_____	a pen
_____	two boxes of pencils	_____	two pens
_____	a box of paper clips	_____	a pencil
_____	two boxes of paper clips	_____	two pencils
_____	a notebook	_____	a pair of scissors
_____	two notebooks	_____	two pairs of scissors

TASK 7

Listen and write the order.

_____	a piece of paper	_____	a paper clip
_____	two pieces of paper	_____	two paper clips
_____	a box of pencils	_____	a pen
_____	two boxes of pencils	_____	two pens and a pencil
_____	a box of paper clips	_____	a pencil
___1___	two boxes of paper clips	_____	two pencils
_____	a notebook	_____	a pair of scissors
_____	two notebooks	_____	two pairs of scissors

TASK 8

Listen and circle.

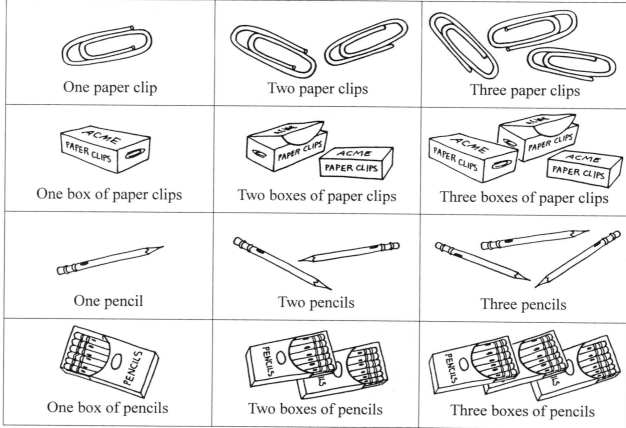

One paper clip	Two paper clips	Three paper clips
One box of paper clips	Two boxes of paper clips	Three boxes of paper clips
One pencil	Two pencils	Three pencils
One box of pencils	Two boxes of pencils	Three boxes of pencils

TASK 9

Listen and circle.

	A	B	C	D
1.	(just one)	two	three	four
2.	just one	two	three	four
3.	just one	two	three	four
4.	just one	two	three	four

TASK 10

Listen and fill in the blanks.

A: _____?

B: _____ I have _____, please?

A: _____?

B: No, _____.

A: _____. Right. What comes next?

B: Could I have _____ and _____?

A: _____?

B: _____. And next, could I have _____ and _____?

A: _____ and _____?

B: _____.

A: Right. _____.

B: _____.

Pair Work: Student A

1. First read to your partner. Then check the answers.

1. two pieces of paper	5. three pair of scissors	9. a box of pencils
2. a paper clip	6. three pieces of paper	10. two notebooks
3. three pens	7. a notebook	11. a pencil
4. two boxes of pencils	8. a box of paper clips	12. a pen

2. First listen to your partner and write the order. Then check the answers.

_____ a piece of paper	_____ two pieces of paper	_____ three pieces of paper
_____ a box of pencils	_____ two boxes of pencils	_____ three boxes of pencils
_____ a box of paper clips	_____ two boxes of paper clips	_____ three boxes of paper clips
_____ a notebook	_____ two notebooks	_____ three notebooks
_____ a paper clip	_____ two paper clips	_____ three paper clips
_____ a pen	_____ two pens	_____ three pens
_____ a pair of scissors	_____ two pairs of scissors	_____ three pairs of scissors
_____ a pencil	_____ two pencils	_____ three pencils

3. Dictate to your partner. Then check the answers.

1. two pens	4. two pairs of scissors	7. a pen
2. a box of paper clips	5. three notebooks	8. two paper clips
3. three pieces of paper	6. a box of pencils	9. a paper clip

4. First listen to your partner and write. Then check the answers.

1. _____
2. _____
3. _____
4. _____
5. _____
6. _____
7. _____
8. _____
9. _____

Pair Work: Student B

1. First listen to your partner and write the order. Then check the answers.

_____ a piece of paper	_____ two pieces of paper	_____ three pieces of paper
_____ a box of pencils	_____ two boxes of pencils	_____ three boxes of pencils
_____ a box of paper clips	_____ two boxes of paper clips	_____ three boxes of paper clips
_____ a notebook	_____ two notebooks	_____ three notebooks
_____ a paper clip	_____ two paper clips	_____ three paper clips
_____ a pen	_____ two pens	_____ three pens
_____ a pair of scissors	_____ two pairs of scissors	_____ three pairs of scissors
_____ a pencil	_____ two pencils	_____ three pencils

2. First read to your partner. Then check the answers.

1.	a pen	5.	three pieces of paper	9.	a box of paper clips
2.	a pencil	6.	two pieces of paper	10.	a box of pencils
3.	a pair of scissors	7.	two paper clips	11.	a piece of paper
4.	three pens	8.	two boxes of pencils	12.	three pairs of scissors

3. First listen to your partner and write. Then check the answers.

1. _____
2. _____
3. _____
4. _____
5. _____
6. _____
7. _____
8. _____
9. _____

4. Dictate to your partner. Then check the answers.

1. a paper clip	4. two boxes of pencils	7. a pair of scissors
2. three boxes of paper clip	5. three pieces of paper	8. three notebooks
3. two notebooks	6. a pen	9. two pencils

12

Another pencil and two more pieces of paper.

Getting Ready

First listen and point. Then listen and repeat.

TASK 1

First listen and point. Then ask and answer the questions with your partner.

Questions
Could I have ...

a box of pencils	another box of pencils	two more boxes of pencils
a pair of scissors	another pair of scissors	two more pairs of scissors
a notebook	another notebook	two more notebooks
a piece of paper	another piece of paper	two more pieces of paper
a pen	another pen	two more pens
a paper clip	another paper clip	two more paper clips

Answers

Sure.	Here.	Of course.	Here you go.

TASK 2

How many? Listen and match the right answers.

1. pairs of scissors   three more
2. pieces of paper   another one
3. pens   just one more
4. notebooks   two more
5. boxes of paper clips   four more
6. paper clips   two

TASK 3

Listen and circle.

	A	B	C
1.	another	another one	just one more
2.	one more	two more	three more
3.	another	just another	just one more
4.	one	one more	another
5.	another one	just two	just two more
6.	three more	four more	six more
7.	seven more	eight more	nine more

TASK 4

Listen and circle.

	A	B	C
1.	(Sure.)	Of course.	Here you go.
2.	Here.	Here you go.	Of course.
3.	Sure.	Here.	Here you go.
4.	Of course.	Sure.	Here.
5.	Sure.	Here.	Here you go.
6.	Here.	Of course.	Here you go.

TASK 5

Slow and fast speech. First listen. Then listen and repeat.

		Slow	*Fast*
1.	another pen	[ænəðɚ pɛn]	[ənəðɚpɛn]
		pen	pen
		another pen	another pen
2.	more pens	[mɔɚ pɛnz]	[mɔɚpɛnz]
		pens	pens
		more pens	more pens
		two more pens	two more pens
3.	could I have	[kʊd aɪ hæv]	[kʊdaɪhæv]
		could I	could I
		could I have	could I have
		Could I have another pen?	Could I have another pen?
4.	how many	[haʊ mɛni]	[haʊmɛni]
		how many	how many
		how many pens	how many pens

TASK 6

Intonation. First listen. Then listen and repeat.

a pencil

a pen and a pencil

a notebook, a pen, and a pencil

a box of paper clips, a notebook, a pen and a pencil

a pair of scissors, a box of paper clips, a notebook, a pen, and a pencil

TASK 7

Listen and write the order.

1. _3_ paper   _1_ pen   _2_ pencil
2. ___ paper   ___ scissors   ___ paper clips
3. ___ paper clips   ___ notebooks   ___ pencils
4. ___ pen   ___ notebook   ___ pencil

TASK 8

Listen and fill in the blanks.

A: Could I have _____, please?

B: _____, here.

A: Thank you. Oh, could I have _____?

B: _____. Here.

A: Thank you. And could I have _____?

B: How many?

A: Two. Two _____.

B: Here you go. Two _____.

A: Thank you.

B: You're welcome.

TASK 9

Listen and fill in the blanks.

A: Could I have _____?

B: _____.

A: And _____. Could I have _____?

B: _____.

A: Thank you. Oh, _____?

B: _____. Here.

A: Could I have _____ and _____, please?

B: _____.

A: _____.

B: _____.

TASK 10

Listen and fill in the blanks.

A: _____ a _____?

B: _____.

A: _____. Oh, _____ have _____, please?

B: _____.

A: Next, _____ boxes _____?

B: _____. Here.

A: Could I _____, please?

B: Right. _____.

A: And _____ box _____.

B: _____. Here.

Pair Work: Student A

1. Tell your partner to write the order. Then check the answers.

1. First, could I have a box of paper clips?
2. Second, could I have a box of pencils?
3. Third, could I have a paper clip and a pencil?
4. Fourth, could I have another box of pencils?
5. Fifth, could I have a piece of paper?
6. Sixth, could I have three more boxes of pencils?
7. Seventh, could I have another box of paper clips?
8. Eighth, could I have another piece of paper?
9. Ninth, could I have four more pieces of paper?
10. Last, could I have one more box of paper clips?

2. Listen to your partner and write the order. Then check the answers.

1. ____ another notebook
2. ____ three more notebook
3. ____ another two paper clips
4. ____ a notebook
5. ____ two more paper clips
6. ____ a piece of paper
7. ____ another pencil
8. ____ four pencils
9. ____ another piece of paper
10. ____ two paper clips

Pair Work: Student B

1. Listen to your partner and write the order. Then check the answers.

1. ____ a paper clip and a pencil
2. ____ another box of paper clips
3. ____ four more pieces of paper
4. ____ a box of paper clips
5. ____ a piece of paper
6. ____ another box of pencils
7. ____ one more box of paper clips

8.   ____   a box of pencils

9.   ____   another piece of paper

10. ____   three more boxes of pencils

2. Tell your partner to write the order. Then check the answers.

1.   First, could I have a notebook?

2.   Second, could I have a piece of paper?

3.   Third, could I have another notebook?

4.   Fourth, could I have four pencils?

5.   Fifth, could I have two paper clips?

6.   Sixth, could I have another two paper clips?

7.   Seventh, could I have another piece of paper?

8.   Eighth, could I have three more notebooks?

9.   Ninth, could I have another pencil?

10. Last, could I have two more paper clips?

13

How many pieces of paper do you have?

Getting Ready

First listen and point. Then listen and repeat.

TASK 1

First listen and point. Then ask and answer the questions with your partner.

TASK 2

Listen and circle.

	A	B
1.	do you want any	do you have any
2.	how many do you want	how many do you have
3.	do you want any more	do you have any more
4.	I don't want any	I don't have any
5.	I want one	I have one
6.	I don't want any more	I don't have any more
7.	I want four more	I have four more

TASK 3

Listen and circle.

A	B	C	D
1. (none)	one	five	nine
2. two	three	ten	twelve
3. eleven	one	seven	nine
4. none	nine	seven	eleven
5. nine	none	one	five
6. eleven	seven	ten	none
7. four	three	five	eight
8. no	none	four	six
9. eleven	any	eight	twenty

TASK 4

Listen and match.

1. books	none
2. boxes	one
3. notebooks	two
4. more notebooks	three
5. pencils	four
6. more pencils	five

TASK 5

Slow and fast speech. First listen. Then listen and repeat.

	Slow	*Fast*
1. do you have	[du yu hæv]	[dəyəhæv]
	do you have	do you have
	Do you have any?	Do you have any?
2. do you want	[du yu want]	[dəyəwan]
	do you want	do you want
	Do you want any?	Do you want any?

3. I have	[aɪ hæv]	[aɪhæv]
	I have	I have
	I have one.	I have one.
4. I don't have	[aɪ dont hæv]	[aɪdonhæv]
	I don't have	I don't have
	I don't have any.	I don't have any.
5. I want	[aɪ want]	[aɪwan]
	I want	I want
	I want one.	I want one.
6. I don't want	[aɪ dont want]	[aɪdonwan]
	I don't want	I don't want
	I don't want any.	I don't want any.

TASK 6

First listen and point. Then listen and circle.

plural:

a blouse	two blouses	a dress	two dresses	[IZ]
a shirt	two shirts	a jacket	two jackets	[S]
a pair of jeans	two pairs of jeans	a sweater	two sweaters	[Z]

TASK 7

Listen and match.

blouses	one
dresses	three
shirts	six
jackets	four
jeans	five
sweaters	two

TASK 8

Listen and fill in the blanks.

1. How many _____ do you _____?
2. How many pairs of _____ do you _____?
3. Do you _____ any _____?
4. Do you _____ another _____?
5. I _____ three _____.
6. I _____ two more _____.
7. How many _____ do you_____?
8. Do you _____ any more _____?

TASK 9

Listen and fill in the blanks.

A: How many _____ do you _____?

B: _____.

A: Do you _____?

B: _____.

A: Do you _____?

B: _____.

A: How many _____?

B: _____.

TASK 10

Listen and fill in the blanks.

A: How many _____?

B: _____.

A: _____?

B: _____.

A: Do you _____?

B: _____ three.

A: Do you _____?

B: _____.

A: How many _____?

B: _____.

Pair Work: Student A

1. **First ask your partner. Then write the answers. Last check your answers.**

   How many _____ do you have?

   ___ blouses   ___ shirts
   ___ dresses   ___ jeans
   ___ jackets   ___ sweaters

2. First listen to your partner and answer the questions. Then check the answers.

Pair Work: Student B

1. First listen to your partner and answer the questions. Then check the answers.

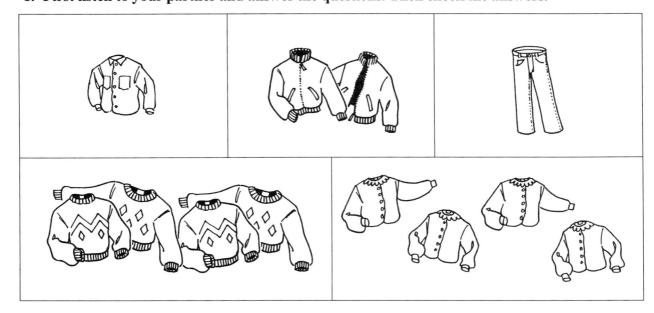

2. First ask your partner. Then write the answers. Last check your answers.

How many _____ do you have?

___ blouses   ___ shirts

___ dresses   ___ jeans

___ jackets   ___ sweaters

14

Sign on the dotted line.

Getting Ready

First listen and point. Then listen and repeat.

93

TASK 1

First listen and point. Then ask and answer the questions with your partner.

First name: _Masao_	First name: _Masao_
Middle name: _____	Middle name: _____
Last name: _Imamura_	Last name: _Imamura_

First name: Mohammed	First name: Mohammed
Middle name: _____	Middle name: _Ali Safir_
Last name: Khan	Last name: Khan

TASK 2

Listen and underline.

A	B	C
1. don't write anything	<u>leave it blank</u>	write them both
2. don't write anything	leave it blank	write them both
3. don't write anything	leave it blank	write them both
4. don't write anything	leave it blank	write them both

TASK 3

Listen and write the order.

   ___ Don't write anything.
   ___ Don't sign anything.
   ___ Don't sign on the line.
   ___ Don't write on the line.
   _1_ Don't sign on the dotted line.
   ___ Don't write on the dotted line.
   ___ Don't sign anything on the line.
   ___ Don't write anything on the line.

TASK 4

Listen and circle.

	A	B	C
1.	(your name)	first name	last name
2.	first name	middle name	last name
3.	first name	middle name	last name
4.	first name	middle name	last name
5.	name	your name	last name
6.	first name	middle name	last name
7.	first name	middle name	last name
8.	your name	first name	last name

TASK 5

Slow and fast speech. First listen. Then listen and repeat.

	Slow	Fast
1. your name	[yuɚ neɪm]	[yɚneɪm]
	your name	your name
	Write your name.	Write your name.
2. your first name	[yuɚ fɚst neɪm]	[yɚ fɚsneɪm]
	your first name	your first name
	Write your first name.	Write your first name.

3. your middle name   [yuɚ mɪdəl neɪm]   [yuɚmɪdlneɪm]

your middle name   your middle name

Write your middle name.   Write your middle name.

4. your last name   [yuɚ læst neɪm]   [yɚ læsneɪm]

your last name   your last name

Write your last name.   Write your last name.

TASK 6

Listen and match.

first line   first line

second line   second line

third line   third line

fourth line   fourth line

fifth line   fifth line

last line   last line

TASK 7

Print   Sign

Kenneth Perry   *Kenneth Perry*

First listen. Then listen again, circle, and match.

1. print/sign   your first name on the last line

2. print/sign   your middle name on the second line

3. print/sign   your last name on the first line

4. print/sign   your name on the line

5. print/sign   your name on the dotted line

TASK 8

First listen and point.

Name:	Hough	David	A.
	(Last)	(First)	(Middle Initial)

Now listen and circle.

1. Name: Becker   Sandra   J.
           (Last)   (First)   (Middle Initial)

2. Name: Satoh   Fumiko
           (Last)   (First)   (Middle Initial)

3. Name: Martinez   Hector   R.
           (Last)   (First)   (Middle Initial)

4. Name: McGill   John   D.
           (Last)   (First)   (Middle Initial)

5. Name: Kramer   Barbara   F.
           (Last)   (First)   (Middle Initial)

TASK 9

Listen and fill in the blanks.

A: First print your _____ on the _____.

B: _____?

A: Right. Next _____ on the _____.

B: On this _____?

A: Yes. Now _____ on the _____.

B: I don't have _____.

A: Then _____ anything. _____ the third line _____.

B: _____ this line _____?

A: Yes. Now, last _____.

B: _____?

A: Yes, _____ your signature.

B: Like this?

A: _____, good.

TASK 10

Listen and fill in the blanks.

A: _____ name _____.

B: _____?

A: Yes. Print your _____, your _____, and _____.

B: I have _____.

A: Print _____.

B: Okay.

A: Good. Now _____ on the _____.

B: _____?

A: _____.

Pair Work: Student A

1. Tell your partner what to write. Then check it.

1. (Print your first name.) _____

2. (Print your last name.) _____

3. (Print your middle name.) _____

4. (Leave this line blank.) _____

5. (Print both your first and last names.) _____

6. (Sign your name.) _

1. (Don't write anything.) _ _ _ _ _

2. (Sign your first name.) _ _ _ _ _

3. (Sign your middle name.) _ _ _ _ _

4. (Sign your last name.) _ _ _ _ _

2. Now listen to your partner and fill in the blanks. Then check your answers.

1. _____

2. _____

3. _____

4. _____

5. _____

6. _

1. _ _ _ _ _ _ _ _ _ _ _ _ _

2. _ _ _ _ _ _ _ _ _ _ _ _ _

3. _ _ _ _ _ _ _ _ _ _ _ _ _

4. _ _ _ _ _ _ _ _ _ _ _ _ _

Pair Work: Student B

1. Listen to your partner and fill in the blanks. Then check the answers.

1. _____   1. _ _ _ _ _ _ _ _ _ _ _

2. _____   2. _ _ _ _ _ _ _ _ _ _ _

3. _____   3. _ _ _ _ _ _ _ _ _ _ _

4. _____   4. _ _ _ _ _ _ _ _ _ _

5. _____

6. _ _ _ _ _ _ _ _ _ _ _ _ _ _ _ _ _ _ _

2. Tell your partner what to write. Then check it.

1. (Leave this line blank.) _____   1. (Print your middle name.) _ _ _ _

2. (Write your last name.) _____   2. (Sign your first name.) _ _ _ _

3. (Sign your last name.) _____   3. (Print your first name.) _ _ _ _

4. (Don't write anything.) _____   4. (Print your middle name.) _ _ _ _

5. (Sign your name.) _____

6. (Write both your first and middle name.) _ _ _ _ _ _ _ _ _ _ _ _ _ _

15

It's on the right.

Getting Ready

First listen and point. Then listen and repeat.

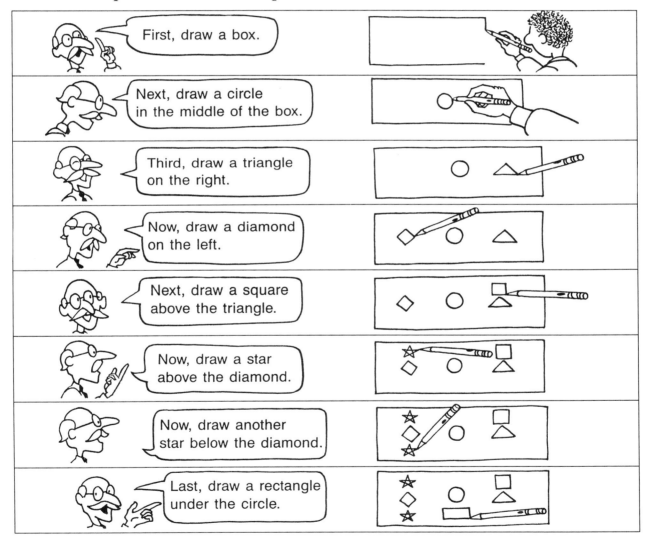

First, draw a box.

Next, draw a circle in the middle of the box.

Third, draw a triangle on the right.

Now, draw a diamond on the left.

Next, draw a square above the triangle.

Now, draw a star above the diamond.

Now, draw another star below the diamond.

Last, draw a rectangle under the circle.

TASK 1

First listen and point. Then practice with your partner.

TASK 2

1. First listen and point.

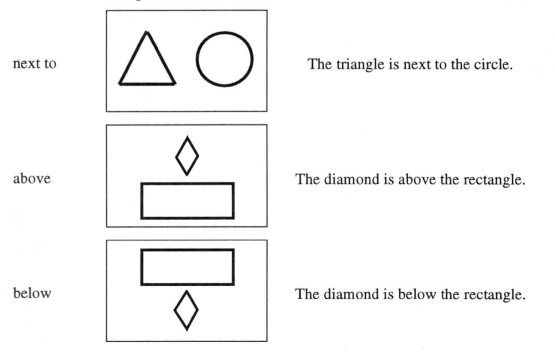

next to — The triangle is next to the circle.

above — The diamond is above the rectangle.

below — The diamond is below the rectangle.

2. Now listen and circle.

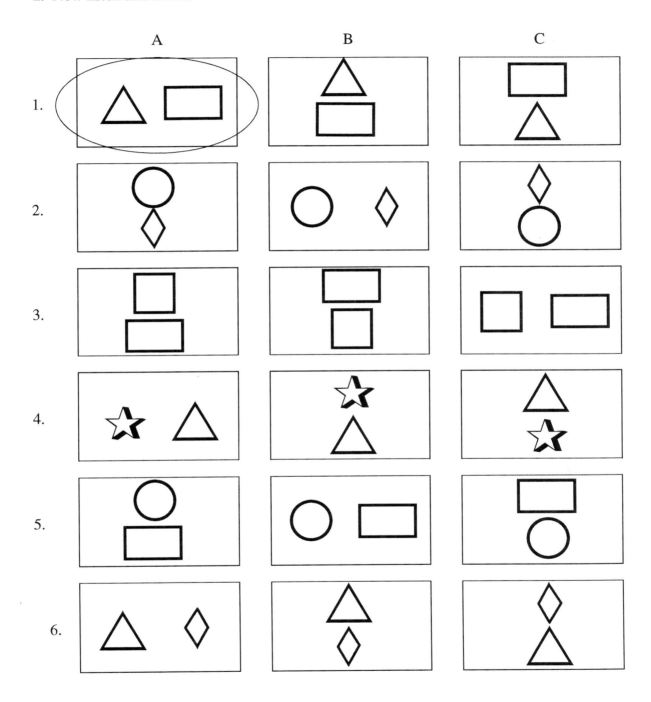

TASK 3

First listen. Then listen and match.

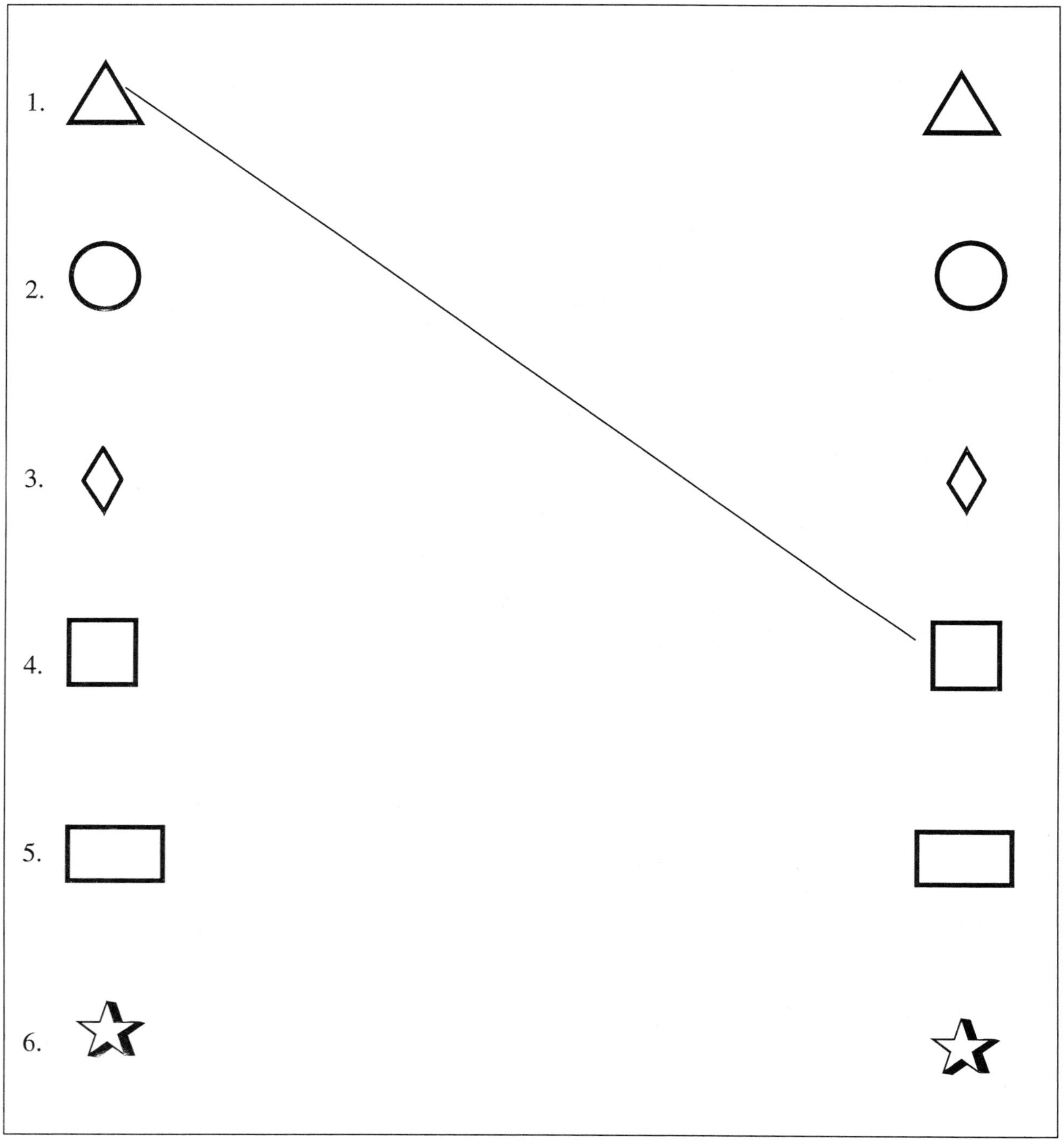

1. △   △

2. ◯   ◯

3. ◇   ◇

4. ☐   ☐

5. ▭   ▭

6. ☆   ☆

TASK 4

Listen and circle.

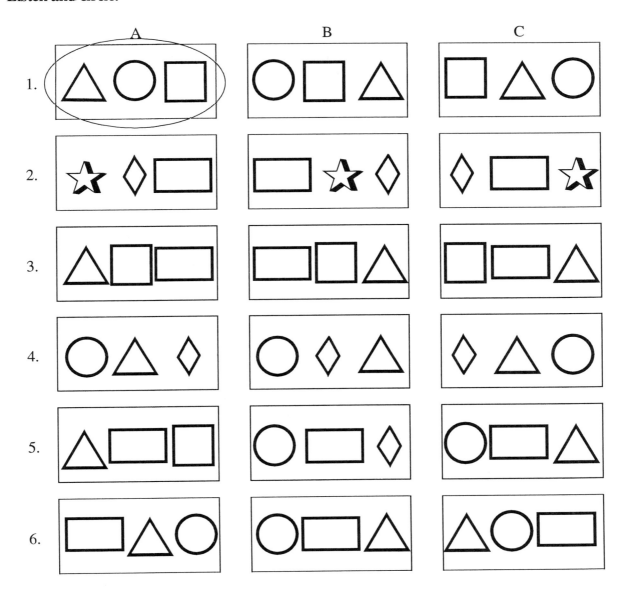

TASK 5

Slow and fast speech. First listen. Then listen and repeat.

		Slow	*Fast*
1.	in the middle	[ɪn ðə mɪdəl]	[ɪnðəmɪdl]
		in the middle	in the middle
		It's in the middle.	It's in the middle.

2. on the right   [an ðə raɪt]   [anðəraɪt]

                                on the right   on the right

                                It's on the right.   It's on the right.

3. on the left   [an ðə lɛft]   [anðəlɛft]

                                on the left   on the left

                                It's on the left.   It's on the left.

4. where is   [wɛɚz]   [wɚz]

                                where is   where's

                                Where is the circle?   Where's the circle?

TASK 6

Listen and fill in the blanks.

A: Where's _____?

B: It's in _____ of the box.

A: Where's _____?

B: It's _____.

A: Where's _____?

B: It's _____.

A: Where's _____?

B: It's _____.

A: Where's _____?

B: It's _____.

TASK 7

Listen and check.

___ Draw another circle below the triangle.   ___ Draw a triangle on the right.

___ Draw a diamond above the circle.   ___ Draw a circle in the middle of the box.

___ Draw another diamond above the circle.   ___ Draw a rectangle on the left.

___ Draw a diamond below the rectangle.   ___ Draw a triangle on the left.

___ Draw another diamond below the rectangle.   ___ Draw a circle on the left.

___ Draw a rectangle on the right.

TASK 8

Listen and follow the directions.

TASK 9

First listen and fill in the blanks. Then listen again and draw in the box below.

1. First _____ a box.
2. _____ draw a _____ in the _____.
3. Now draw a _____ the _____.
4. And then draw a _____ next to the _____ on the _____.
5. Next draw a _____ next to the _____ on the _____.
6. And now draw a _____ below the _____.
7. Now draw _____ below the _____.
8. Last draw a _____ below the _____.

TASK 10

First listen and fill in the blanks. Then listen again and draw in the box below.

1. First _____.

2. Second draw a _____.

3. Third draw a _____ on _____.

4. Next draw a _____ the triangle.

5. Now draw a _____.

6. And then draw a _____.

7. Last draw a _____.

Pair Work: Student A

1. **Look at the picture below. Tell your partner what to draw. Then check the drawing.**

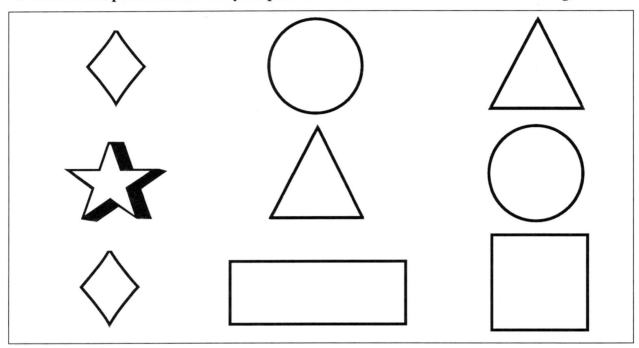

2. **Listen to your partner and follow the directions. Then check the drawing.**

Pair Work: Student B

1. Listen to your partner and follow the directions. Then check the drawing.

2. Look at the picture below. Tell your partner what to draw. Then check the drawing.

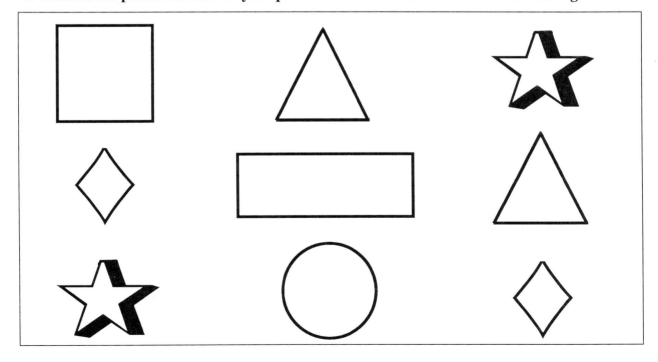

16

Follow the directions.

Getting Ready

First listen and point. Then listen and repeat.

TASK 1

First listen and point. Then practice with your partner.

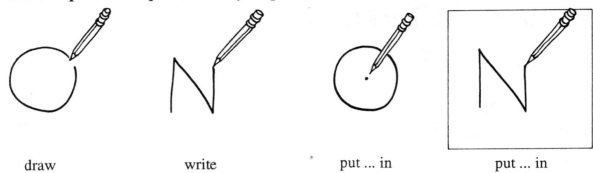

draw   write   put ... in   put ... in

TASK 2

Listen and circle.

an   *a*

an A	an M	a B	a Q
an E	an N	a C	a T
an F	an O	a D	a U
an H	an R	a G	a V
an I	an S	a J	a W
an L	an X	a K	a Y
		a P	a Z

TASK 3

Listen and check the right box.

	A		B		C	
1.	write	✔	draw	☐	take out	☐
2.	put	☐	draw	☐	write	☐
3.	sign	☐	write	☐	put	☐
4.	draw	☐	take out	☐	write	☐
5.	put	☐	sign	☐	draw	☐
6.	write	☐	put	☐	draw	☐
7.	sign	☐	put	☐	write	☐
8.	draw	☐	sign	☐	write	☐
9.	take out	☐	put	☐	write	☐
10.	sign	☐	take out	☐	draw	☐

TASK 4

Listen and circle.

	A	B	C
1.	(a dot)	a check	a question mark
2.	an X	a circle	a check
3.	a square	a rectangle	a triangle
4.	a diamond	a star	a dot
5.	a check	an X	a box
6.	a rectangle	a triangle	a circle
7.	a question mark	a diamond	a star
8.	an N	a check	a question mark

TASK 5

Slow and fast speech. First listen. Then listen and repeat.

		Slow	*Fast*
1.	write a	[raɪt ə]	[raɪdə]
		write a	write a
		Write a D.	Write a D.
		Write a U.	Write a U.
2.	write an	[raɪt ən]	[raɪtn]
		write an	write an
		Write an X.	Write an X.
		Write an F.	Write an F.
3.	on the line	[an ðə laɪn]	[ənðəlaɪn]
		on the line	on the line
		Write on the line.	Write on the line.
4.	in the	[ɪn ðə]	[ənðə]
		in the	in the
		in the circle	in the circle
		in the square	in the square

TASK 6

Listen and match.

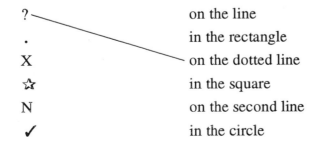

?	on the line
.	in the rectangle
X	on the dotted line
☆	in the square
N	on the second line
✓	in the circle

TASK 7

Listen and follow the directions.

1. _____
2. _____
3. _____
4. _____
5. _____
6. _____

TASK 8

Listen and fill in the blanks.

A: Are you ready?

B: _____.

A: Okay. Listen and _____ the _____.

B: _____.

A: First _____ a _____.

B: Okay.

A: Now _____ on the _____, a _____ in the middle, and a
_____ on the _____.

B: Like this?

A: Right. Next put a _____ in the _____ on the _____.

B: Here?

A: Good. Now put a _____ in the _____.

B: A _____?

A: Yes. And last _____ an _____ in the _____.

B: Okay.

A: _____.

TASK 9

Listen and fill in the blanks.

A: _____ my _____. Are you _____?

B: _____.

A: Okay. First, _____ a _____ and a _____.

B: _____.

A: Good. Now _____ three _____.

B: Like this? One..., two..., three.

A: Yes. Next, _____ on the _____ and a _____ on the _____.

B: A _____ and a _____.

A: _____. Now _____ an _____ on the _____ line.

B: _____?

A: No, an _____. _____ as in _____.

B: _____ as in _____?

A: Right. Next, _____ a _____ in the _____ of the _____ on the _____ line.

B: Here?

A: Yes, good. And _____ put a _____ in the _____ on the _____.

TASK 10

Listen and fill in the blanks.

A: _____, take out _____.

B: Okay.

A: Good. Now _____.

B: Right, _____.

A: Okay. Next, _____.

B: Like this?

A: Yes. Now _____ on the _____ line.

B: On the _____?

A: No, on the _____.

B: Right, on the _____.

A: Next, _____ and _____ on the _____, and _____ on the _____.

B: Okay.

A: Last, _____ a _____ in the _____, a _____ in the
   _____ and an _____ in the _____. And _____ show me
   _____.

Pair Work: Student A

1. Look at the picture below and tell your partner what to write. Then check the picture.

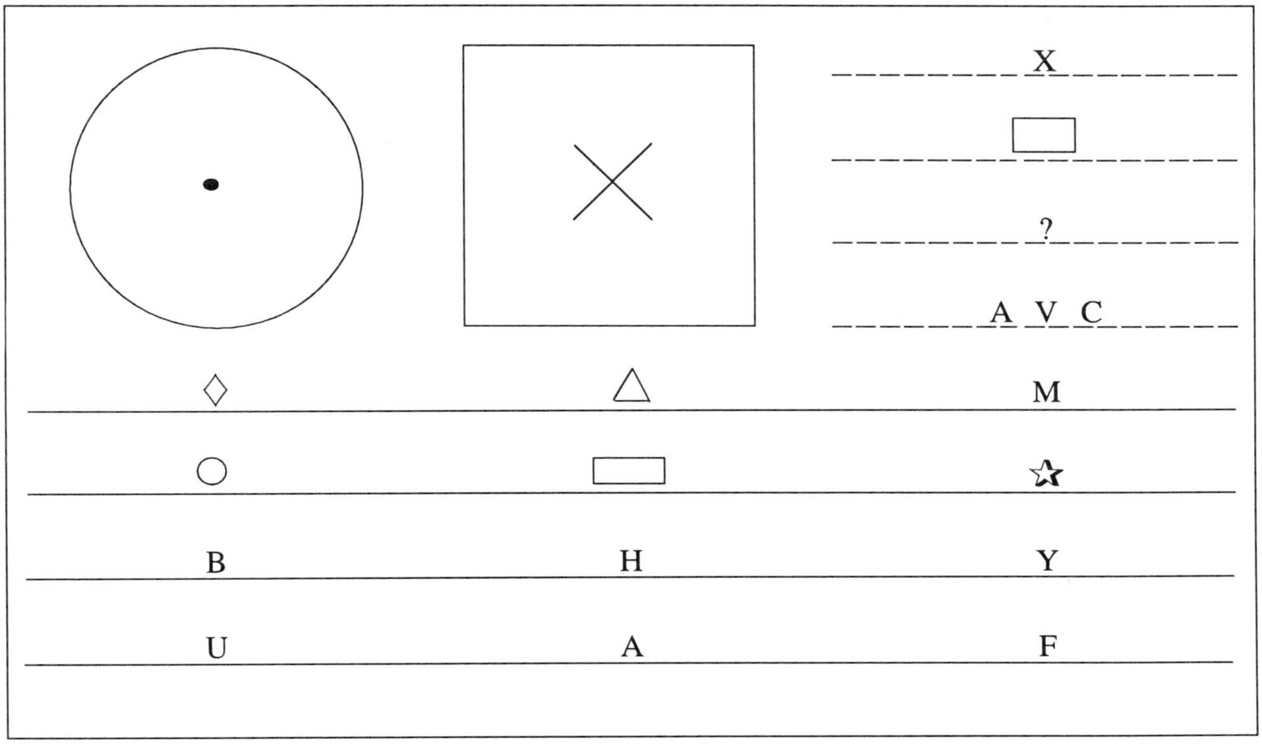

2. Listen to your partner and follow the directions. Then check the picture.

Pair Work: Student B

1. **Listen to your partner and follow the directions. Then check the picture.**

2. Look at the picture below and tell your partner what to draw. Then check the picture.

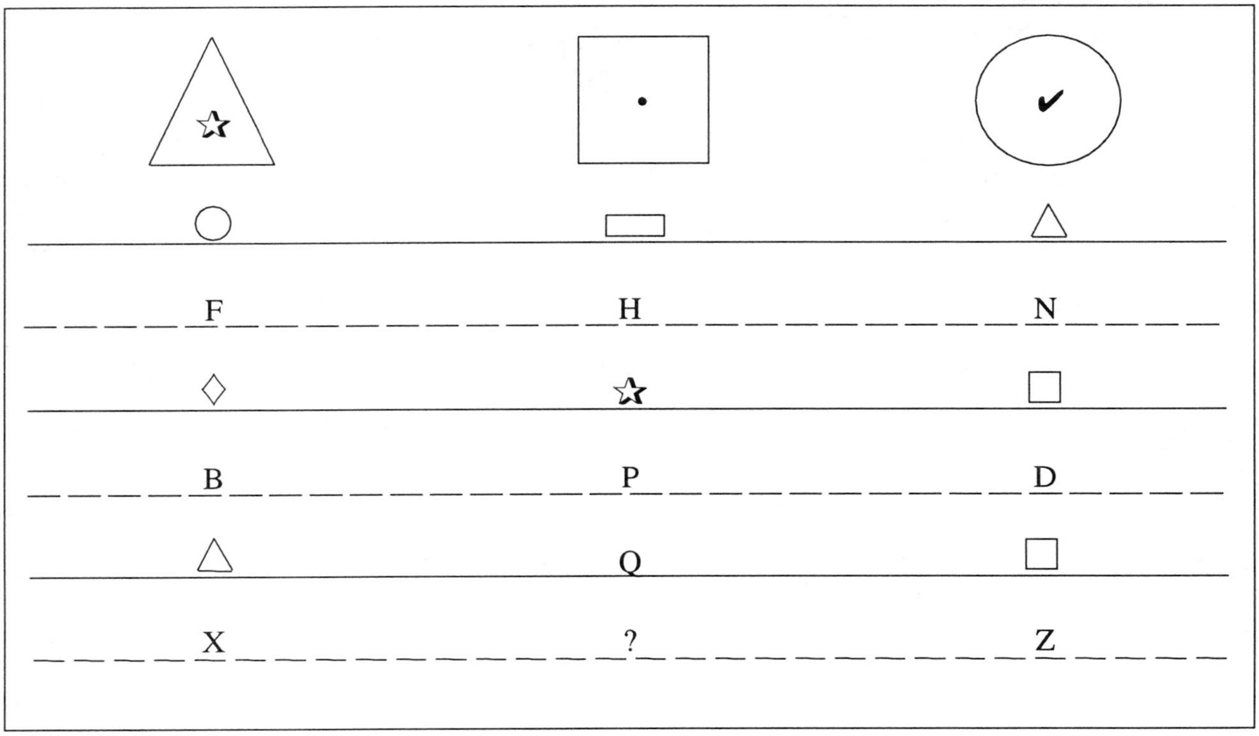

F   H   N

◇   ☆   □

B   P   D

△   Q   □

X   ?   Z

17

Mark the date on your calendar.

Getting Ready

First listen and point. Then listen and repeat.

Sunday	Monday	Tuesday	Wednesday	Thursday	Friday	Saturday
	1	②	3	4	5	6
7	8	9	10	11	12	13
14	15	16	⑰	18	19	20
21	22	23	24	㉕	26	27
28	29	30	31			

TASK 1

Look at the calendar again. First listen and point. Then practice with your partner.

TASK 2

First listen and point. Then listen and mark.

Days:	Dates:				
Sunday	the 1st	the 8th	the 15th	the 22nd	the 29th
Monday	the 2nd	the 9th	the 16th	the 23rd	the 30th
Tuesday	the 3rd	the 10th	the 17th	the 24th	the 31st
Wednesday	the 4th	the 11th	the 18th	the 25th	
Thursday	the 5th	the 12th	the 19th	the 26th	
Friday	the 6th	the 13th	the 20th	the 27th	
Saturday	the 7th	the 14th	the 21st	the 28th	

TASK 3

Listen and mark an X in the box next to the days of the week.

1.	Sunday	☐	Monday	☒	Friday	☐
2.	Tuesday	☐	Thursday	☐	Saturday	☐
3.	Wednesday	☐	Friday	☐	Monday	☐
4.	Wednesday	☐	Monday	☐	Sunday	☐
5.	Saturday	☐	Wednesday	☐	Friday	☐
6.	Thursday	☐	Saturday	☐	Tuesday	☐
7.	Tuesday	☐	Wednesday	☐	Thursday	☐
8.	Thursday	☐	Wednesday	☐	Tuesday	☐

TASK 4

First listen and point. Then listen and mark the months.

Months

January (1)	February (2) ✔	March (3)	April (4)	May (5)	June (6)
July (7)	August (8)	September (9)	October (10)	November (11)	December (12)

	A	*B*	*C*
1.	January	February	March
2.	March	May	June
3.	April	August	July
4.	September	October	November
5.	October	November	December
6.	June	May	March
7.	July	April	August
8.	September	December	January

TASK 5

Slow and fast speech. First listen to the days and dates. Then listen and repeat.

		Slow	*Fast*
1.	Sunday	[səndeɪ]	[səndi]
	day	Sunday	Sunday
	date	Sunday, the 2nd	Sunday, the 2nd
2.	Monday	[məndeɪ]	[məndi]
	day	Monday	Monday
	date	Monday, the 6th	Monday, the 6th
3.	Tuesday	[tuzdeɪ]	[tuzdi]
	day	Tuesday	Tuesday
	date	Tuesday, the 13th	Tuesday, the 13th

4. Wednesday   [wɛnzdeɪ]   [wɛnzdi]

    day   Wednesday   Wednesday

    date   Wednesday, the 17th   Wednesday, the 17th

5. Thursday   [θɚzdeɪ]   [θɚzdi]

    day   Thursday   Thursday

    date   Thursday, the 20th   Thursday, the 20th

6. Friday   [fraɪdeɪ]   [fraɪdi]

    day   Friday   Friday

    date   Friday, the 28th   Friday, the 28th

7. Saturday   [sætɚdeɪ]   [sætɚdi]

    day   Saturday   Saturday

    date   Saturday, the 31st   Saturday, the 31st

TASK 6

First listen and point. Then listen and repeat.

Calendar Years

1900	nineteen hundred		2000	two thousand
1901	nineteen oh-one		2009	twenty oh-nine
1912	nineteen twelve		2010	twenty ten
1923	nineteen twenty-three		2021	twenty twenty-one
1934	nineteen thirty-four		2032	twenty thirty-two
1945	nineteen forty-five		2043	twenty forty-three
1956	nineteen fifty-six		2054	twenty fifty-four
1967	nineteen sixty-seven		2065	twenty sixty-five
1978	nineteen seventy-eight		2076	twenty seventy-six
1989	nineteen eighty-nine		2087	twenty eighty-seven
1990	nineteen ninety		2098	twenty ninety-eight

Now look at the years again. Listen and write the date.

1. _____   4. _____   7. _____

2. _____   5. _____   8. _____

3. _____   6. _____   9. _____

TASK 7

Listen and circle the years.

1900	1920	1940	1960	1980	2000	2020	2040	2060	2080
1901	1921	1941	1961	1981	2001	2021	2041	2061	2081
1902	1922	1942	1962	1982	2002	2022	2042	2062	2082
1903	1923	1943	1963	1983	2003	2023	2043	2063	2083
1904	1924	1944	1964	1984	2004	2024	2044	2064	2084
1905	1925	1945	1965	1985	2005	2025	2045	2065	2085
1906	1926	1946	1966	1986	2006	2026	2046	2066	2086
1907	1927	1947	1967	1987	2007	2027	2047	2067	2087
1908	1928	1948	1968	1988	2008	2028	2048	2068	2088
1909	1929	1949	1969	1989	2009	2029	2049	2069	2089
1910	1930	1950	1970	1990	2010	2030	2050	2070	2090
1911	1931	1951	1971	1991	2011	2031	2051	2071	2091
1912	1932	1952	1972	1992	2012	2032	2052	2072	2092
1913	1933	1953	1973	1993	2013	2033	2053	2073	2093
1914	1934	1954	1974	1994	2014	2034	2054	2074	2094
1915	1935	1955	1975	1995	2015	2035	2055	2075	2095
1916	1936	1956	1976	1996	2016	2036	2056	2076	2096
1917	1937	1957	1977	1997	2017	2037	2057	2077	2097
1918	1938	1958	1978	1998	2018	2038	2058	2078	2098
1919	1939	1959	1979	1999	2019	2039	2059	2079	2099

TASK 8

Listen and match.

Sunday   the 1st
Monday   December 1st
Tuesday   the 11th
Wednesday   March 11th
Thursday   the 17th
Friday   October 17th

TASK 9

Look at the calendar below. Listen and circle the dates.

Sunday	Monday	Tuesday	Wednesday	Thursday	Friday	Saturday
	1	2	3	4	5	6
7	8	9	10	11	12	13
14	15	16	17	18	19	20
21	22	23	24	25	26	27
28	29	30	31			

TASK 10

Listen and fill in the blanks.

A: _____ at the _____.

B: Okay.

A: What _____ is the _____?

B: It's _____.

A: Okay, _____ that date on your _____.

B: _____.

A: Right. Next, what day is the _____?

B: It's _____.

A: _____ it on your _____.

B: _____.

A: Last, what day _____?

B: _____.

A: _____.

B: Right. _____.

Pair Work: Student A

1. **Look at the calendar below and answer your partner's questions. Then check the answers.**

Sunday	Monday	Tuesday	Wednesday	Thursday	Friday	Saturday
					1	2
3	4	5	6	7	8	9
10	11	12	13	14	15	16
17	18	19	20	21	22	23
24	25	26	27	28	29	30
31						

2. **Ask your partner to answer your questions. Write the answers. Then check your answers with your partner.**

What day is the 11th?   It's Saturday.

Saturday the 11th

_____   _____

_____   _____

_____   _____

_____   _____

Pair Work: Student B

1. **Ask your partner to answer your questions. Write the answers. Then check your answers with your partner.**

What day is the 17th?   It's Sunday.

Sunday the 17th   _____

_____   _____

_____   _____

_____   _____

_____

Look at the calendar below and answer your partner's questions. Then check the answers.

Sunday	Monday	Tuesday	Wednesday	Thursday	Friday	Saturday
			1	2	3	4
5	6	7	8	9	10	11
12	13	14	15	16	17	18
19	20	21	22	23	24	25
26	27	28	29	30	31	

18

Write the date in the upper right-hand corner.

Getting Ready

First listen and point. Then listen and repeat.

TASK 1

First listen and point. Then practice with your partner.

a △   the other △

a ○   another ○   the other ○

a □   another □   another □   the other □

TASK 2

Listen and circle.

	A	B	C
1.	(a)	another	the other
2.	a	another	the other
3.	a	another	the other
4.	a	another	the other
5.	a	another	the other
6.	a	another	the other
7.	a	another	the other

TASK 3

Listen and write the order. Mark an X next to any wrong answer.

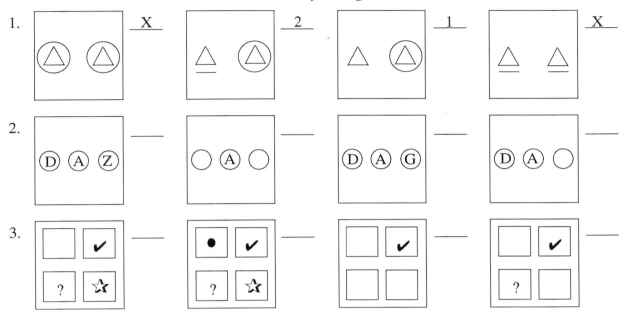

TASK 4

Listen and circle the right dates.

A	B	C
1. August 2, 1996	August 7, 1996	August 2, 1998
2. April 13, 2030	April 30, 2014	April 13, 2013
3. December 1, 1989	December 4, 1989	December 5, 1989
4. September 25, 2009	September 26, 2019	September 26, 2009
5. March 7, 1922	March 11, 1972	March 2, 1972
6. October 12, 1999	September 12, 1990	November 12, 1995
7. January 3, 2001	January 2, 2010	January 3, 2011
8. February 2, 1949	February 7, 1999	February 7, 2029

TASK 5

Slow and fast speech. First listen. Then listen and repeat.

		Slow	*Fast*
1.	August 2	[ɔgəst sɛkənd]	[ɔgəsɛkn]
		August the 2nd	August 2nd
		August the 2nd, 1997	August 2nd, 1997
2.	between...and	[bitwin...ɛnd]	[bətwin...n]
		between 1 and 10	between 1 'n 10
		between 1995 and 1999	between 1995 'n 1999
3.	in the corner	[ɪn ðə kɔɚnɚ]	[ənðə kɔnɚ]
		in the corner	in the corner
		in the upper right-hand corner	in the upper right-hand corner
		in the lower left-hand corner	in the lower left-hand corner

TASK 6

Listen and match

1. Jan. 1, 1995   April 1, 2011
2. May 10, 1998   June 17, 2023
3. Aug. 25, 2010   Dec. 18, 1996
4. March 21, 2019   July 6, 1999
5. Nov. 11, 2007   Oct. 30, 2007
6. Feb. 7, 1999   Sept. 13, 2011

TASK 7

Listen and check the right answer.

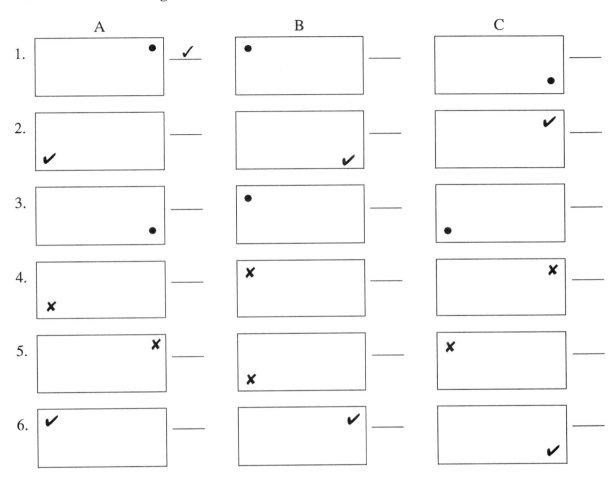

TASK 8

Listen and match.

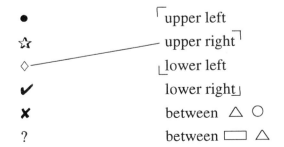

TASK 9

Listen and fill in the blanks.

A: Write _____ in the _____-hand _____.

B: Here.

A: Right. Next write _____ in the _____-hand _____.

B: In the _____?

A: Right. Now put an _____ in the _____-hand _____.

B: The _____-hand _____?

A: Yes. And _____ a _____ in the _____-hand _____.

B: The _____?

A: Right. Next _____ a _____ on the line _____.

B: Like this?

A: Right. Now _____ a _____ on the line _____.

B: A _____ on the line _____.

A: Good. Last _____ a _____ between the _____.

B: Here?

A: That's right.

TASK 10

Listen and follow the directions.

Pair Work: Student A

1. Look at the picture below. Tell your partner what to fill in. Then check it.

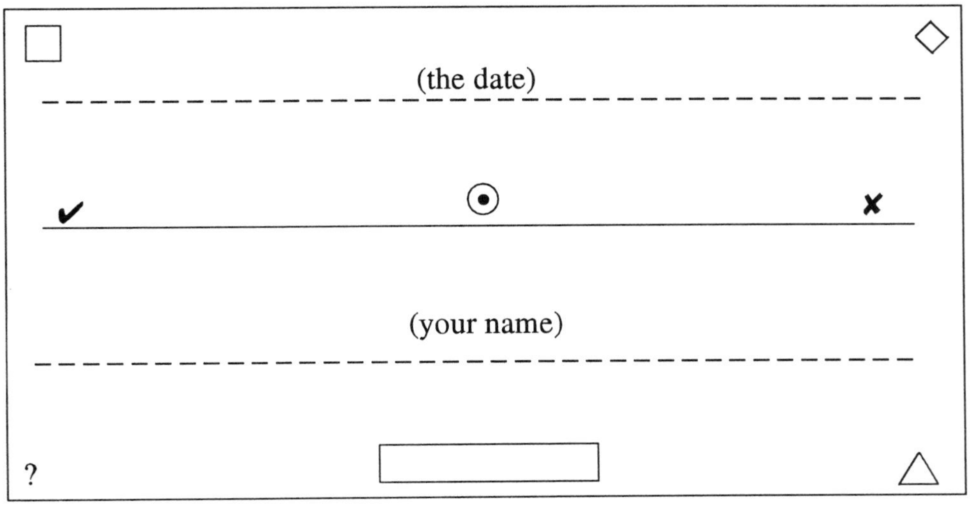

☐   ◇

--------------------------- (the date) ------------------------

✔   ⊙   ✘
_____

(your name)

- -

?   [   ]   △

2. Listen to your partner and follow the directions. Then check.

_____

- -

_____

Pair Work: Student B

1. Listen to your partner and follow the directions. Then check.

2. Look at the picture below. Tell your partner what to fill in. Then check it.

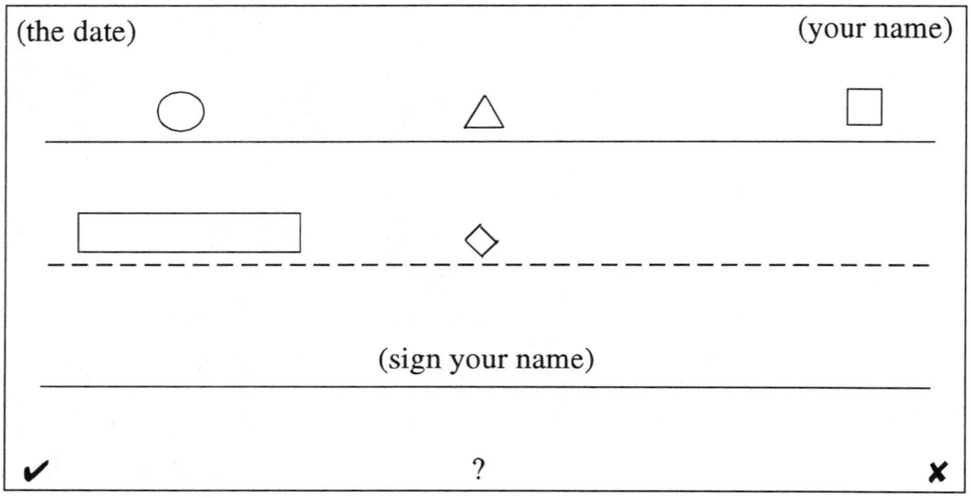

(the date)   (your name)

(sign your name)

✔   ?   ✘

19

What day is tomorrow?

Getting Ready

First listen and point. Then listen and repeat.

Calendar ~ May						
Sunday	Monday	Tuesday	Wednesday	Thursday	Friday	Saturday
		1	2	3	4	5
6	PARTY 7	8	CLASS 9	GAME 10	11	12

the day before yesterday   yesterday   today   tomorrow   the day after tomorrow

Look at the calendar. What day is tomorrow?

Tomorrow is Wednesday. We have class.

Okay. Class tomorrow. What day is the baseball game?

The game is the day after tomorrow.

Okay. Thursday. What's the date?

It's May 10th.

Thursday is May 10th. And what day is the party?

The party? Yesterday. It was yesterday!

the party   class   the baseball game

TASK 1

First listen and point. Then practice with your partner.

What day was _____?	What day is _____?
yesterday the day before yesterday	today tomorrow the day after tomorrow
What was the date?	What is the date?

Calendar ~ May						
Sunday	Monday	Tuesday	Wednesday	Thursday	Friday	Saturday
13	14	15	16	17	18	19

TASK 2

First look at the calendar. Then listen and match the days and dates below.

Sunday	Monday	Tuesday	Wednesday	Thursday	Friday	Saturday
1	2 a week ago Monday	3 a week ago Tuesday	4 a week ago Wednesday	5 a week ago Thursday	6 last Friday	7 last Saturday
8 last Sunday	9 last Monday	10 last Tuesday	11 the day before yesterday	12 yesterday	(13) today	14 tomorrow
15 the day after tomorrow	16 this Monday	17 this Tuesday	18 this Wednesday	19 this Thursday	20 next Friday	21 next Saturday

1. today   was the 4th
2. last Monday   was the 9th
3. this Tuesday   is the 13th
4. last Saturday   was the 7th
5. the day after tomorrow   is the 17th
6. a week ago Wednesday   is the 20th
7. next Friday   is the 15th

TASK 3

Look at the calendar above again. Listen and circle the dates.

TASK 4

Listen and circle.

	A	B	C
1.	last	(this)	next
2.	last	this	next
3.	last	this	next
4.	last	this	next
5.	last	this	next
6.	last	this	next
7.	last	this	next

TASK 5

Slow and fast speech. First listen. Then listen and repeat.

		Slow	Fast
1.	is	[ɪz]	[z]
		today is	today's
		Today is the 5th.	Today's the 5th.
2.	was	[wəz]	[wəz]
		was	was
		yesterday was	yesterday was
		Yesterday was Monday.	Yesterday was Monday.
3.	before	[bifɔɚ]	[bəfɔɚ]
		before	before
		the day before	the day before
		the day before yesterday	the day before yesterday
4.	after	[æftɚ]	[æftɚ]
		after	after
		the day after	the day after
		the day after tomorrow	the day after tomorrow

TASK 6

Listen and check the right box.

1	2	3	4	5	6	7	8
☐ is	☐ is	☐ is	☐ is	☐ is	☐ is	☐ is	☐ is
☑ was	☐ was	☐ was	☐ was	☐ was	☐ was	☐ was	☐ was

TASK 7

Listen and fill in the blanks.

1. What day _____?
2. _____ the game _____?
3. _____ Wednesday.
4. _____ the day _____?
5. _____ Friday _____ the 6th.
6. _____ the 13th.
7. _____ the 17th.
8. _____ the 22nd?

TASK 8

Listen and fill in the blanks.

A: _____ the calendar.

B: What _____?

A: _____. We have class.

B: What _____?

A: _____ the day _____.

B: Okay, _____. What's Thursday's date?

A: _____.

B: Right. _____. And what _____?

A: The _____? _____. It _____.

TASK 9

Listen and match.

the party   the third Monday in January

the baseball game   the day after tomorrow

Memorial Day   the last Monday in May

Martin Luther King Day   the first Monday in September

Labor Day   this Saturday

TASK 10

Listen and mark your calendar.

today		the game		the party

Discovery Day		Canada Day

June						
Sunday	Monday	Tuesday	Wednesday	Thursday	Friday	Saturday
May 28	29	30	31	June 1	2	3
4	5	6	7	8	9	10
11	12	13	14	15	16	17
18	19	20	21	22	23	24
25	26	27	28	29	30	July 1

Pair Work: Student A

1. **Ask your partner when these holidays are. Mark them on your calendar. Then check your answers.**

U.S. Holidays

New Year's Day	Labor Day
Martin Luther King Day	Columbus Day
President's Day	Veteran's Day
Memorial Day	Thanksgiving Day
Independence Day	Christmas Day

2001

January
S	M	T	W	T	F	S
	1	2	3	4	5	6
7	8	9	10	11	12	13
14	15	16	17	18	19	20
21	22	23	24	25	26	27
28	29	30	31			

February
S	M	T	W	T	F	S
				1	2	3
4	5	6	7	8	9	10
11	12	13	14	15	16	17
18	19	20	21	22	23	24
25	26	27	28			

March
S	M	T	W	T	F	S
				1	2	3
4	5	6	7	8	9	10
11	12	13	14	15	16	17
18	19	20	21	22	23	24
25	26	27	28	29	30	31

April
S	M	T	W	T	F	S
1	2	3	4	5	6	7
8	9	10	11	12	13	14
15	16	17	18	19	20	21
22	23	24	25	26	27	28
29	30					

May
S	M	T	W	T	F	S
		1	2	3	4	5
6	7	8	9	10	11	12
13	14	15	16	17	18	19
20	21	22	23	24	25	26
27	28	29	30	31		

June
S	M	T	W	T	F	S
					1	2
3	4	5	6	7	8	9
10	11	12	13	14	15	16
17	18	19	20	21	22	23
24	25	26	27	28	29	30

July
S	M	T	W	T	F	S
1	2	3	4	5	6	7
8	9	10	11	12	13	14
15	16	17	18	19	20	21
22	23	24	25	26	27	28
29	30	31				

August
S	M	T	W	T	F	S
			1	2	3	4
5	6	7	8	9	10	11
12	13	14	15	16	17	18
19	20	21	22	23	24	25
26	27	28	29	30	31	

September
S	M	T	W	T	F	S
						1
2	3	4	5	6	7	8
9	10	11	12	13	14	15
16	17	18	19	20	21	22
23	24	25	26	27	28	29
30						

October
S	M	T	W	T	F	S
	1	2	3	4	5	6
7	8	9	10	11	12	13
14	15	16	17	18	19	20
21	22	23	24	25	26	27
28	29	30	31			

November
S	M	T	W	T	F	S
				1	2	3
4	5	6	7	8	9	10
11	12	13	14	15	16	17
18	19	20	21	22	23	24
25	26	27	28	29	30	

December
S	M	T	W	T	F	S
						1
2	3	4	5	6	7	8
9	10	11	12	13	14	15
16	17	18	19	20	21	22
23	24	25	26	27	28	29
30	31					

2. **Answer your partner's questions. Then check the answers.**

Canadian Holidays

New Year's Day	Jan. 1
New Year's Day Observance	Jan. 2
Victoria Day	the third Monday in May
Discovery Day	the fourth Monday in June
Canada Day	July 1
Labor Day	the first Monday in September
Thanksgiving Day	the first Monday in October
Remembrance Day	Nov. 11
Christmas Day	Dec. 25
Boxing Day	Dec. 26

Pair Work: Student B

1. **Answer your partner's questions. Then check the answers.**

U.S. Holidays

New Year's Day	Jan. 1
Martin Luther King Day	the third Monday in January
President's Day	the third Monday in February
Memorial Day	the last Monday in May
Independence Day	July 4
Labor Day	the first Monday in September
Columbus Day	the second Monday in October
Veteran's Day	Nov. 11
Thanksgiving Day	the fourth Thursday in November
Christmas Day	Dec. 25

2. **Ask your partner when these holidays are. Mark them on your calendar. Then check your answers.**

Canadian Holidays

New Year's Day	Labor Day
New Year's Day Observance	Thanksgiving Day
Victoria Day	Remembrance Day
Discovery Day	Christmas Day
Canada Day	Boxing Day

2002

January

S	M	T	W	T	F	S
		1	2	3	4	5
6	7	8	9	10	11	12
13	14	15	16	17	18	19
20	21	22	23	24	25	26
27	28	29	30	31		

February

S	M	T	W	T	F	S
					1	2
3	4	5	6	7	8	9
10	11	12	13	14	15	16
17	18	19	20	21	22	23
24	25	26	27	28		

March

S	M	T	W	T	F	S
					1	2
3	4	5	6	7	8	9
10	11	12	13	14	15	16
17	18	19	20	21	22	23
24	25	26	27	28	29	30
31						

April

S	M	T	W	T	F	S
	1	2	3	4	5	6
7	8	9	10	11	12	13
14	15	16	17	18	19	20
21	22	23	24	25	26	27
28	29	30				

May

S	M	T	W	T	F	S
			1	2	3	4
5	6	7	8	9	10	11
12	13	14	15	16	17	18
19	20	21	22	23	24	25
26	27	28	29	30	31	

June

S	M	T	W	T	F	S
						1
2	3	4	5	6	7	8
9	10	11	12	13	14	15
16	17	18	19	20	21	22
23	24	25	26	27	28	29
30						

July

S	M	T	W	T	F	S
	1	2	3	4	5	6
7	8	9	10	11	12	13
14	15	16	17	18	19	20
21	22	23	24	25	26	27
28	29	30	31			

August

S	M	T	W	T	F	S
				1	2	3
4	5	6	7	8	9	10
11	12	13	14	15	16	17
18	19	20	21	22	23	24
25	26	27	28	29	30	31

September

S	M	T	W	T	F	S
1	2	3	4	5	6	7
8	9	10	11	12	13	14
15	16	17	18	19	20	21
22	23	24	25	26	27	28
29	30					

October

S	M	T	W	T	F	S
		1	2	3	4	5
6	7	8	9	10	11	12
13	14	15	16	17	18	19
20	21	22	23	24	25	26
27	28	29	30	31		

November

S	M	T	W	T	F	S
					1	2
3	4	5	6	7	8	9
10	11	12	13	14	15	16
17	18	19	20	21	22	23
24	25	26	27	28	29	30

December

S	M	T	W	T	F	S
1	2	3	4	5	6	7
8	9	10	11	12	13	14
15	16	17	18	19	20	21
22	23	24	25	26	27	28
29	30	31				

20

When does the movie start?

Getting Ready

First listen and point. Then listen and repeat.

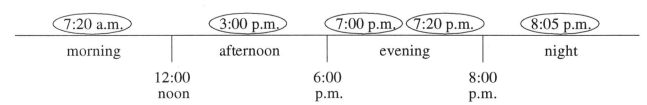

TASK 1

First listen and point. Then practice with your partner.

When		class	When		it
	does	the meeting			class
		the movie		does	the meeting finish?
What time		the game	What time		the movie
					the game
	10:30	in the morning		10:30	in the morning
	2:00	afternoon		12:00	noon
It starts at	6:00	evening	It finishes at	2:00	afternoon
	8:00	at night		6:00	evening
				8:00	at night

TASK 2

First listen and match. Then listen and circle.

1:05 ⟍   twelve twenty

12:20   three fifteen

3:15   ⟍ one oh-five

A	B	C
1. (1:15)	1:50	1:05
2. 6:30	2:15	6:13
3. 5:40	9:40	9:20
4. 7:30	7:20	7:15
5. 8:35	8:45	8:55
6. 3:05	3:15	3:25

TASK 3

Listen and underline.

A	B	C	D
1. start	starts	finish	finishes
2. start	starts	finish	finishes
3. start	starts	finish	finishes
4. start	starts	finish	finishes
5. start	starts	finish	finishes
6. start	starts	finish	finishes

TASK 4

First listen and point. Then listen and circle.

a quarter after one	= 1:15
half past one	= 1:30
a quarter to two	= 1:45

	a quarter after	half past	a quarter to
1.	1:15	1:30	(1:45)
2.	2:15	2:30	2:45
3.	3:15	3:30	3:45
4.	4:15	4:30	4:45
5.	5:15	5:30	5:45
6.	6:15	6:30	6:45

TASK 5

Slow and fast speech. First listen. Then listen and repeat.

		Slow	*Fast*
1.	at	[æt]	[ət']
		at	at
		at 9:30	at 9:30
2.	a quarter to	[ə kwɔtɚ tu]	[əkwɔdɚdə]
		a quarter to	a quarter to
		a quarter to ten	a quarter to ten
3.	a quarter after	[ə kwɔtɚ æftɚ]	[ə kw,dɚæftɚ]
		a quarter after	a quarter after
		a quarter after six	a quarter after six
4.	half past	[hæf pæst]	[hæfpæs]
		half past	half past
		half past noon	half past noon

TASK 6

Listen and circle.

	yesterday	today	tomorrow
1.	yesterday morning	(this morning)	tomorrow morning
2.	yesterday at noon	today at noon	tomorrow at noon
3.	yesterday afternoon	this afternoon	tomorrow afternoon
4.	yesterday evening	this evening	tomorrow evening
5.	last night	tonight	tomorrow night

TASK 7

Listen and circle.

	A	*B*	*C*
1.	at	in the	(this)
2.	at	in the	this
3.	at	in the	this
4.	at	in the	this
5.	at	in the	this
6.	at	in the	this

TASK 8

Listen and fill in the blanks.

A: When does class _____?

B: _____.

A: _____?

B: No, _____.

A: When _____?

B: _____.

A: When's your _____ with Ken?

B: Tomorrow _____.

A: _____?

B: _____.

A: And the party?

B: Saturday _____.

TASK 9

First listen and point. Then listen and match.

breakfast	lunch	dinner
with Ken	with Fumiko	with Remi
from 7 to a quarter to 8	from noon to one	from half past six to 8

1. your breakfast with Masao   6:00-7:30

2. your meeting with Sandra   10:00-11:20

3. your lunch with Fereshteh   9:00-9:45

4. your meeting with Sirikit   5:30-6:20

5. your dinner with Setsi   12:00-1:30

6. your meeting with Jun   6:00-7:45

TASK 10

Listen and fill in the blanks.

A: When is _____?

B: It _____ in the morning and _____.

A: When is _____?

B: Lunch is _____ o'clock.

A: When is _____ Carol?

B: It's from _____ to _____.

A: And _____ Paul?

B: That's _____. It _____ and _____.

A: When is _____?

B: _____. From _____ to _____.

Pair Work: Student A

1. Look at the calendar and answer your partner's questions. Then check the answers.

Monday, March 11 A.M.	Tuesday, March 12 A.M.
8	8
9 9:00-10:30 class	9 9:00-10:30 class
10 10:45-12:00 meeting with the teacher	10
11	11 11:00-12:15 meeting with Hector
P.M.	**P.M.**
12 12:00-1:00 lunch with Elani	12 12:30-1:30 lunch with Nguyen
1	1
2 2:20-4:00 meeting with Francis	2
3	3 3:45 baseball game
4 4:40-5:15 meeting with Gloria	4
5	5
6 6:30 dinner with Gunther	6 6:00 dinner with Charles
7 7:35 movie	7
8	8 party

2. Ask your partner when these are. Write your answers in the calendar below. Then check your answers.

breakfast with Ulani	your meeting with Julo
the game	your meeting with Carlos
the movie	your meeting with Jun
class	your meeting with Joran
dinner with Fumiko	lunch with Boris
dinner with Yvette	your lunch with Ahmed

Wednesday, November 11	Thursday, November 12
A.M.	**A.M.**
8	8
9	9
10	10
11	11
P.M.	**P.M.**
12	12
1	1
2	2
3	3
4	4
5	5
6	6
7	7
8	8

Pair Work: Student B

1. **Ask your partner when these are. Write your answers in the calendar below. Then check your answers.**

your meeting with Francis	dinner with Gunther
your meeting with Hector	dinner with Charles
your meeting with Gloria	class
your meeting with the teacher	the party
lunch with Nguyen	the movie
lunch with Elani	the baseball game

Monday, March 11 A.M.	Tuesday, March 12 A.M.
8	8
9	9
10	10
11	11
P.M.	P.M.
12	12
1	1
2	2
3	3
4	4
5	5
6	6
7	7
8	8

2. Look at the calendar and answer your partner's questions. Then check the answers.

Wednesday, November 11
A.M.
8
9   9:10-10:40 meeting with Carlos
10   10:50-11:45 meeting with Joran
11
P.M.
12   12:15-12:50 lunch with Ahmed
1
2   2:30-4:30 game
3
4
5
6   6:00-7:30 dinner with Fumiko
7
8   8:00-9:55 movie

Thursday, November 12
A.M.
8   8:00-9:15 breakfast with Ulani
9   9:40-10:30 meeting with Jun
10   10:45-12:00 meeting with Julo
11
P.M.
12   12:30-2:00 lunch with Boris
1
2
3
4
5
6   6:00-7:00 dinner with Yvette
7   7:20-8:05 class
8

21

What's seven and fifteen?

Getting Ready

First listen and point. Then listen and repeat.

7 + 8 plus	9 + 5 and	7 plus <u>15</u> is 22
3 and <u>+12</u> is 15	4 plus <u>+5</u> equals 9	6 and <u>+2</u> equals 8
9 – 7 minus	20 minus <u>– 4</u> is 16	14 minus <u>–10</u> equals 4

TASK 1

First listen. Then listen and fill in the blanks.

7 +5	15 +30	70 − 9
72 −23	19 +90	60 −16

A: What's _____ plus _____?

B: _____.

A: Right. What's _____ and _____?

B: _____ and _____?

A: No, _____ and _____.

B: It's _____.

A: Right. What's _____ minus _____?

B: _____ minus _____?

A: No, _____ minus _____.

B: _____.

A: Very good.

Now practice with your partner.

TASK 2

Listen and circle and answers.

	A	B	C
1.	3	(13)	30
2.	11	21	71
3.	19	64	90
4.	43	60	63
5.	32	67	85

TASK 3

Listen and circle the answers.

	A	B	C
1.	(6)	16	60
2.	13	15	50
3.	30	50	60
4.	16	30	63
5.	1	5	9

TASK 4

Listen and check the questions.

1. 14 + 12 ✓	14 – 12	14 + 20
2. 70 + 30	70 – 30	70 – 13
3. 80 – 18	80 + 18	18 + 18
4. 10 + 12	20 – 10	10 + 20
5. 40 + 54	40 – 14	14 + 40
6. 17 – 16	70 – 60	70 – 16
7. 66 – 26	66 + 14	66 – 40
8. 82 – 60	82 – 16	82 + 60

TASK 5

Slow and fast speech. First listen. Then listen and repeat.

	Slow	*Fast*
1. and	[ɛnd]	[n]
	and	'n
	What is seven and twelve?	What's 7 and twelve?
2. is	[ɪz]	[z]
	nine is	nine's
	Nine and four is thirteen.	Nine 'n four's thirteen.

3. is

[ɪz]
six is
Ten minus six is four.

[əz]
six's
Ten minus six's four.

4. is

[ɪz]
eight is
Seven plus eight is
  fifteen.

[s]
eight's
Seven plus eight's
  fifteen.

TASK 6

Listen and circle.

A	B	C
1. 10	(33)	90
2. 14	15	40
3. 12	20	4
4. 28	54	80
5. 28	78	81

TASK 7

Listen and circle.

A	B	C
1. (+)	−	=
2. +	−	=
3. +	−	=
4. +	−	=
5. +	−	=

TASK 8

Listen and match.

1.	$12 - 5 = 7$	4.	$40 - 14 = 26$
2.	$28 + 12 = 40$	5.	$17 + 40 = \ ?$
3.	$50 + 14 = 64$	6.	$60 - 42 = 18$

TASK 9

Listen and fill in the blanks.

A: What's _____?

B: _____ and _____?

A: No, _____.

B: It's _____.

A: Right.

B: What's _____?

A: _____.

B: Right.

TASK 10

Listen and fill in the blanks.

1. _____ + _____ = _____
2. _____ – _____ = _____
3. _____ = _____
4. _____ = _____
5. _____
6. _____

Pair Work: Student A

1. **First tell your partner where to write the question. Then ask your partner the question. After your partner has answered all the questions, check the answers.**

   a. What's twelve + seven?

   b. What's twenty + fourteen?

   c. What's sixty – sixteen?

   d. What's seven + twenty–five?

   e. What's forty–eight – twelve?

   f. What's eighty–three – eleven?

   g. What's sixty – eight?

   h. What's fifty–four + nineteen?

   i. What's twenty – nineteen?

i.   b.   e.

g.   a.   c.

d.

f.

h.

2. First write down the question where your partner tells you to. Then write the answer to the question. Last check your answers.

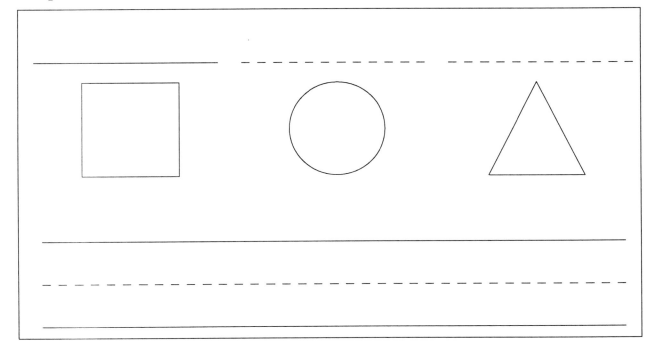

Pair Work: Student B

1. **First write down the question where your partner tells you to. Then write the answer to the question. Last check your answers.**

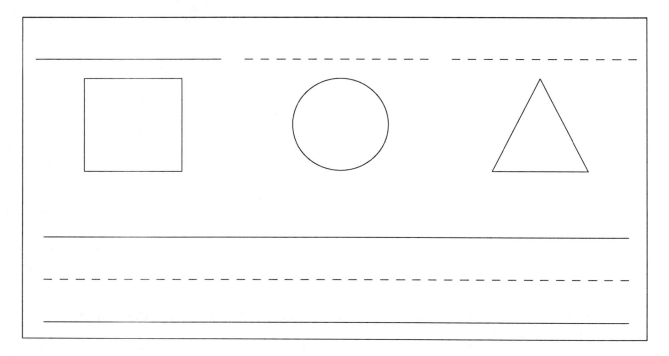

2. First tell your partner where to write the question. Then ask your partner the question. After your partner has answered all the questions, check the answers.

a. What's six – seventeen?

b. What's fifteen + fifty?

c. What's twenty–nine + fourteen?

d. What's thirty – sixteen?

e. What's thirty + forty?

f. What's sixty–six – twenty–four?

g. What's ninety – eighteen?

h. What's seventeen – nine?

i. What's eighty + eighteen?

22

How much is eight times thirty?

Getting Ready

First listen and point. Then listen and repeat.

How much is eight times thirty?

It's two-hundred forty.

$8 \times 30 = 240$

How much is seven into thirty-five?

It's five.

$7\overline{)35} = 5$

And how much is eighty-one divided by nine?

Divided by . . .?

$81 \div 9 = 9$

Divided by nine. 81 divided by nine.

Okay, it's nine.

Right. And what's six times fifteen?

Six times fifty?

No, six times fifteen.

It's ninety.

Right.

$6 \times 15 = 90$

TASK 1

First listen and point. Then listen and fill in the blanks.

$12\overline{)144}$	10×13	$14\overline{)28}$
50×15	$40 \div 5$	19×70

A: What's _____ into _____?

B: _____.

A: Right. What's _____ times _____?

B: It's _____.

B: That's right. And what's _____ into _____?

B: Two.

A: Good. And how much is _____ times _____?

B: It's _____.

A: Okay. And what's _____ divided by _____?

B: _____.

A: And how much is _____ times _____?

B: It's _____.

Now practice with your partner.

TASK 2

Listen and circle and answers.

	A	B	C
1.	14	(40)	140
2.	15	50	150
3.	6	16	60
4.	18	9	92
5.	7	17	700

TASK 3

Listen and circle and the answers.

	A	B	C
1.	(5)	60	65
2.	17	70	270
3.	92	2	19
4.	15	50	515
5.	22	12	16

TASK 4

Listen and check the questions.

1.	$7\overline{)14}$ ✓	7×14	$40 \div 7$
2.	$30 \div 6$	30×6	13×6
3.	$44 \div 11$	$4\overline{)44}$	$11\overline{)44}$
4.	$116 \div 4$	4×16	29×4
5.	14×7	$7\overline{)14}$	$98 \div 7$
6.	6×6	6×36	$6\overline{)36}$

TASK 5

Slow and fast speech. First listen. Then listen and repeat.

	Slow	*Fast*
1. times seven	[taɪmz sɛvɛn] times seven thirteen times seven	[taɪmsɛvn] times seven thirteen times seven
2. divided by	[dɪvaɪdəd baɪ] divided by	[dəvaɪdədbaɪ] divided by
3. into	[ɪntu] into two into twelve	[əndə] into two into twelve

4. how much is	[hau mətʃ ɪz]
	how much is
	how much is seven
	  and six?
		[haʊmətʃəz]
		how much's
		how much's seven
		  'n six?

TASK 6

Listen and fill in the blanks.

A: How much is _____?

B: It's _____.

A: How much is _____?

B: It's _____.

A: And how much is _____?

B: Divided _____?

A: Divided _____. _____.

B: Okay, it's _____.

A: Right. And _____?

B: _____ times _____?

A: No, _____.

B: It's _____.

A: Right.

TASK 7

Listen and check.

	A	B	C
1.	×	÷	)‾
2.	×	÷	)‾
3.	×	÷	)‾
4.	×	÷	)‾
5.	×	÷	)‾

TASK 8

Listen and match.

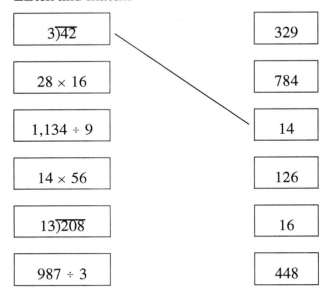

3)42̄	329
28 × 16	784
1,134 ÷ 9	14
14 × 56	126
13)208̄	16
987 ÷ 3	448

TASK 9

Listen and fill in the boxes.

1.	2.	3.
_____ × _____ = _____	+ _____	− _____
4.	**5.**	**6.**
_____ ÷ _____ = _____	)‾‾‾‾‾‾	
7.	**8.**	**9.**

TASK 10

Listen and fill in the blanks.

A: How much is _____ and _____?

B: It's _____.

A: Write the answer in _____ on _____.

B: Okay.

A: Good. Next, what's _____ minus _____?

B: It's _____.

A: Okay. Write your answer _____. Now what's _____ times _____?

B: _____ times _____ is _____.

A: Good. Write your _____ on _____.

B: What's next?

A: How much is _____?

B: _____.

A: Okay. Write your _____.

Pair Work: Student A

1. **First tell your partner where to write the question. Then ask your partner the question. After your partner has answered all the questions, check the answers.**

   a. $89 + 44$ d. $165 - 72$ g. 20×13

   b. $45 \div 9$ e. $13\overline{)65}$ h. 15×30

   c. 13×50 f. $27 - 18$ i. $44 + 100$

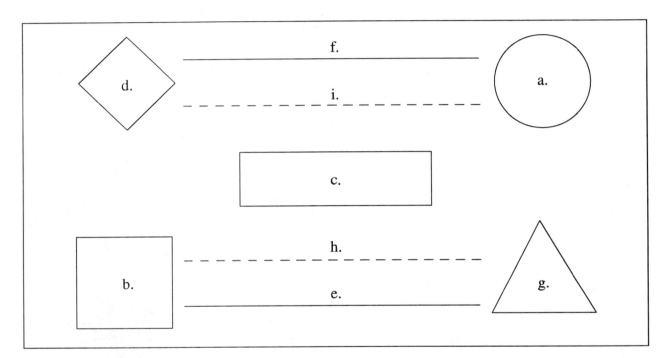

2. **First write down the question where your partner tells you to. Then write the answer to the question. Last check your answers.**

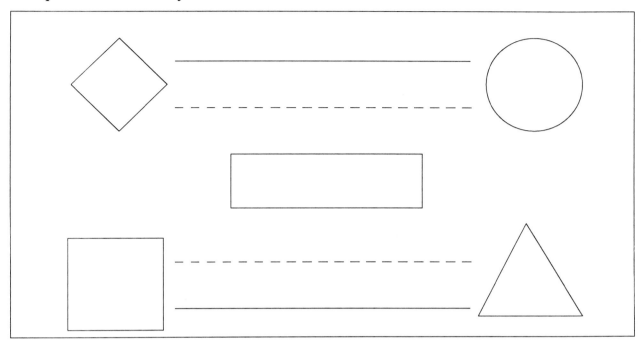

Pair Work: Student B

1. **First write down the question where your partner tells you to. Then write the answer to the question. Last check your answers.**

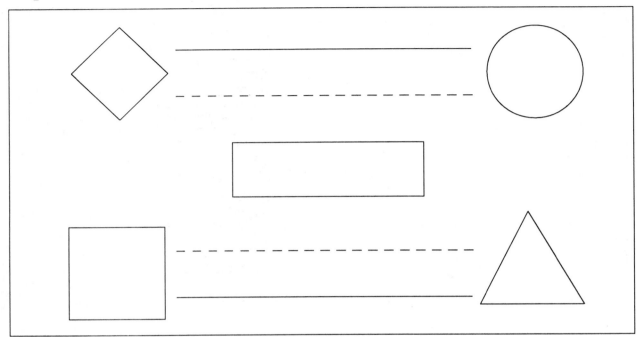

2. First tell your partner where to write the question. Then ask your partner the question. After your partner has answered all the questions, check the answers.

a. 17×6 d. $35 - 19$ g. $36 \div 6$

b. 16×7 e. $16)\overline{144}$ h. $85 \div 5$

c. $94 + 37$ f. $120 - 85$ i. $970 + 13$

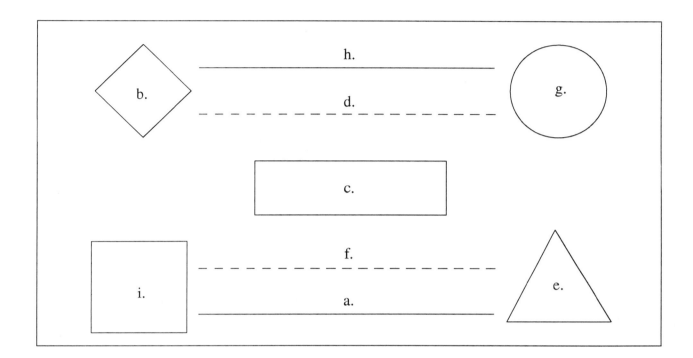